OMG!

Why The Hell Have You Forsaken Us?

WHERE ANGELS FEAR TO TREAD

OMG!

Why The Hell Have You Forsaken Us?

WHERE ANGELS FEAR TO TREAD

Jêan Németh

WAKEMAN
PUBLISHING
ENLIGHTENING INFORMATION

enquiries: wakemanpublishing@jeannemeth.com

"I write as a citizen of the world who serves no ruler. Early I lost my fatherland only to exchange it for the wide world..."

Friedrich Schiller 1759-1805

Acknowledgments

I wish to acknowledge the many *Bearers Of Light,* who have dared to venture *Where Angels Fear To Tread*: inventors, researchers, scientists, presenters, teachers, leaders, healers, writers, artisans, philosophers, including mothers, fathers and everyday people not always recognized for their deeds, and those upon whom we have bestowed the title of *avatar* for their inspired philosophical insights in various cultures and faiths over millennia, who have lived —sometimes endured— many lifetimes to bring light to our world.

Jêan Németh 2008

My Dearest Leyna

You have been a light that has guided and inspired me to aim for my highest potential, the darkness that has embraced and nurtured me during times of introspection and solitude. You are *A Bearer Of Light.*

Excerpt from Journal

A Cry To The Universe

I've been asking questions all my life and now I damn well want some answers! God hasn't replied to my call and I'm sick and tired of waiting. I invoke, no, I demand a reply from anyone or anything out there in the ethers that can hear me. I don't care where the answer comes from, whether it's from my higher consciousness, guides, angels, cherubs, nymphs, gnomes, elementals, little green men from Mars, fairies at the bottom of the garden, dead relatives or anyone else who is willing to listen. I just don't care!

Why is it that everything in which I try to succeed and manifest in my life fizzles out, falls by the wayside or seems to be condemned to a miserable failure before I even start? Yes, I admit that procrastination is one of my weak points, but I do eventually follow through on all that I say I am going to do, including all the things I'm supposed to do: I meditate, I pray, I connect with my higher consciousness, I try to have conversations with God, I talk to my guides, I use positive affirmation and manifestation techniques and open myself to the limitless abundance of the universe and all it has to offer. I even ask for the support of the archangels!

My desire to succeed in life and my belief in my ability to be able do so, has been a strong focus since I was 14, now the numbers are reversed for God's sake—and still I haven't been able to bring about that ever-elusive manifestation of my hopes, dreams and wishes, and let me tell you, it's not for want of trying!

I've been doing this for years and I'm sick and tired of repeating the same cycle over and over again; broken dreams and promises that never get fulfilled. I've become cynical and bored with all the spiritual and philosophical platitudes from writings that only generate temporary insight, but never give the full answer or remedy. I've participated in meditation and discussion groups, listened to and watched a myriad of CD's, DVD's and read enough material on spirituality and information on mind and manifestation techniques to fill an entire library and I've had enough! As ye sow, so shall ye also reap, preaches one school of thought, Ask and it is given, says another—so where are the damned results? Apparently my salvation lies in the power of now moment, but it truly must be the secret of all time 'cause I still haven't been able to crack it!

Why is it that everything I do seems destined to fail? Why can't I make my own philosophy work for me? Where the hell have I gone wrong? Is my karma so heavy and dark that I'm being blocked at every turn? What is it with this restriction grid that seems to be limiting my every attempt at achieving my hopes, dreams and wishes? AM I CURSED ?

If there is such a thing, I claim my universal right and entitlement to make my "one call" from this prison planet, and I ask... no, I demand that someone answer me NOW!

Atonement

I stared at the blinking cursor on my laptop without any expectation. Worse, I felt no better for having vented my frustrations. I knew there would be no answer, no reply from anyone. How could there be? The entire universe was just a cold, empty, dark heartless black hole, where random, meaningless happenings affected all sentient beings unfortunate enough to be inflicted with self-awareness.

I sat there brooding, like an adolescent not having gotten his way, but it didn't take long before I was overcome with grief.

How had I come to this? Why had I allowed a few setbacks and disappointments in my life to make me so angry? What did I have to complain about? I was fortunate enough to be in a happy, loving relationship with my beloved wife who is my soul partner. I was fit and healthy, never having experienced any serious illness or disease. I didn't live in a country ravaged by war, famine or starvation. All in all, my life was very comfortable, yet why did I feel such an emptiness inside, so unfulfilled in my personal life?

Reading back I felt ashamed: my questions and demands seemed selfish verging on narcissistic. What about our troubled world? What about the pain and suffering endured by countless souls every second of every day? How dare I feel sorry for myself! But then, wasn't that part of why I felt so angry? Why does the human condition have to consist of so much pain, suffering and frustration?

"What are we doing here?" I yelled, exasperated. "Where the hell's the sense in it all? I do want some answers damn it! And not from someone else's experience either, but from my own! Direct communion! Isn't that what we're told we can all have?" I waited, glaring at the ceiling.

I slammed shut my laptop. Clearly, I was one jaded soul, cynical and sick of life's frustrations. I threw my hands into the air, "You're all a pack of cowards! There are no guides. There are no angels watching over us. There is no purpose to it all. There is no God! It's all just an illusion, a grand story we've been sold and stupidly bought. It's just a big fat lie and as far as my so-called spiritual path goes, I quit!"

As I stood up to exit the study, electricity suddenly charged the air. I felt disorientated, unsure of what was happening as the energy dominated the room. I swore I could hear a sound, imagining it to be the whoosh of gigantic feathered wings. I was struck by the awareness of a presence, invisible yet pervasive. Nothing materialized... but then again, nothing ever does!

I turned to leave the room, when I heard the words of a softly spoken voice, 'So, you really believe there's no purpose to it all?' It was calm and pleasant, not to my ear, but rather to my mind! Although it was coming from all around, I was sure it was my imagination, another trick of the flawed human psyche... just another disillusioning experience.

'And, *it's just a big fat lie*, you say?'

Startled, I fell backward down onto the chair. There was an edge of authority, yet there was no distinct gender to the tone.

'Open your laptop, place your fingers on the keyboard and listen carefully.'

The Dialogue Begins...

One

Are you truly open to anyone answering your call?

Yeah, sure I am. I'll play along.

"Playing along" has indeed been your game-play of recent times. Do you think you can spare the time to truly *hear* the answers you are seeking?

Why not? I've got nothing better to do. And you are?

I am "The Bearer of Light".

"The Bearer of Light". Really? Are you one of my guides?

I have guided you at times.

Well I've been asking for one of you guys to make

1

yourself known to me for years. What took you so long?

You have never actually asked for *my* particular presence, but I have tried to get your attention from time to time.

You feel familiar. Have you spoken to me in my meditations before?

In a manner of speaking—

Surely you come under one of the guises listed in my journaling exercise.

It was your invitation to *anyone* answering your call that opened a corridor of communication. You're usually more cautious in such invocations.

So, maybe you're just an energy-sucking vampire who preys on the emotions of disillusioned souls. I just wanted a response from *someone*!

Well, here I am.

Great! Then show yourself.

Before we continue, are you sure that you want all your questions answered?

Gee! Let me think about that—of course I want my questions answered! Would you please show yourself?

I am already in your presence.

Where?

Everywhere.

Oh I see. You're one of those *omnipresent* types. Next, I suppose you'll tell me that you're God and you want me to take notes. Well, unless God suffers from senility he'd know that that's already been done.

—

Hello! Anyone there?

God, as the Deity and Creator of the universes, is an unfathomable cosmic jewel with infinite facets. I am but one.

What's with the cryptic lingo?

Listen with your heart and all will be revealed.

Here we go! I hope you're not going to give me the usual "*you have all the answers within*" stuff,

3

because I'm over all that. I want some plain non-double-entendre answers to some very clear and straightforward questions.

Do you know how many years I've been meditating, connecting with spirit, opening myself to higher guidance and yet I've had no real response. Where the hell have you been all this time?

Is there a reason why you are yelling?

I'm not yelling! I'm writing.

Perhaps you could write a little less loudly. Communication through the medium of telepathy is a very sensitive affair.

Maybe it's because I'm angry! I've got several issues with life and all its frustrations and hardship.

Most of you do.

Trying to make sense of, and deal with this crazy world we live in is enough to drive you round the bend. Particularly when nothing ever seems to work out. I just want some clear answers.

Perhaps I can be of assistance.

Just don't give me a sermon. I'm not impressed with religion and men running round in frocks with their "holier than thou" attitude either.

Religion as it currently stands certainly does lean on the side of Patriarchy.

What's the point of the Church pretending to have answers and solutions to question they very well know no longer suit the modern world? They tell us to continue having faith during hard times, while their coffers are full of priceless treasures, their institution controls major banks—and then have the audacity to suggest that self-punishment and martyrdom is what God intended for his world full of sinners! Have you ever heard anything more self-indulgent?

Believe me, I'd be the last one to give you a sermon. But please, keep going. Your own example of self-indulgence is absolutely riveting.

I consider myself a bit of a freethinker, but even the New Age, Spiritual, Esoteric and Metaphysical movements are beginning to annoy me. I'm over all the philosophical jargon and platitudes that only generate temporary insight and relief, but never really give the complete answer or remedy.

Well, hell's below! I certainly didn't expect your emotional floodgates to open with such gusto so soon.

"Hell's below!" What do you mean by that?

Heaven's above! Only hindsight will give you insight to this humor.

You really must be careful that your anger doesn't lead to bitterness. Repressed emotions will almost always lead to disease, which is of course merely a side effect of the core issue: *fear of...*

Well maybe if you'd spent most of your life believing that you were going to achieve something wonderful, have it confirmed by countless psychics, and then discover that at every turn you're blocked, you'd be slightly pissed off as well. And yes, suddenly waking up and realizing that the years have slipped by, while you were so busy trying to "make it" you didn't even notice, would be enough to annoy the hell out of anyone!

At 14 I'd planned to make it by the time I was 18! And here I am, the numbers reversed, working two casual jobs, living on the edge, still waiting for the seemingly elusive dream of success to become a reality. What the hell happened? Where did I take the wrong turn?

Your concept of *making it* merely comes from a limited perception of not being able to see the overall picture. There are no *wrong* turns, just choices with lots of variable outcomes.

Those "choices" I made don't look so good in hindsight.

That depends on "where you're at" at the time and what you are looking back on!

Why connect with me now? I've been asking for guidance during my meditation for years. You've left your run a bit too late!

Communications have been made with you since you were born, but you chose not to be too good a listener. Guidance has got you to where you are now. There is no real delay, just a better timing waiting to unfold. You agreed to fulfill a mission before you came back, the content of which would only be made available to you when the time was right within the scheme of things and when you were ready to listen. That time is now.

Really! What if you're just my alter ego playing some kind of psychological mind game?

7

What if you're just a man fortunate enough to be having a personal experience of *inspired writing*?

What if I'm just having yet another early mid-life-crisis or more likely a nervous breakdown?

Personally, I think you'd be great as a Shake-spearean actor. Dramatics seems to be your central theme.

What's with the wisecracks?

Just mirroring your lead.

I thought a guide from the other side would be *taking* the lead and *setting* the example.

Been there, done that. Special cases need special treatment. You know what they say, if you can't beat'em—

What do you want from me?

If you allow your mind to open, I'm going to assist you in expanding your perceptions about life and purpose on a personal and mass level.

Allow my mind to open! Open to what? A voice in my head! We have medical terms for that kind of behavior. In the past it was called possession! For all I know you could be some kind of demon trying to influence me, a soul-collector for Satan.

I've been accused of all of the above, and oh so much more, since time immemorial. But seriously, you should put that imagination of yours to good use. Ever thought of writing?

Was that supposed to be funny? If you know anything about me—

Yes, I know your story. You're a talented, imaginative and frustrated singer, writer and overall thespian who has lost his faith and believes he has been blocked at every turn and wonders whether his life has been nothing but a big fat failure.

I wouldn't have put it quite that strongly—

Deal with it! It's time to face your fears.

Well, I have been blocked... haven't I?

From your linear perspective you could say—

I knew it! It's as if there is some kind of energy field around me, a *restriction grid*, a curse of some kind. But why? "Ask and yea shall receive" goes the saying. Well I've been asking for as long as I can remember.

Do you know how many books I've read on manifestation techniques and put into practice over the years? Why haven't I been able to bring my hopes, dreams and wishes to reality? With all the energy I've put in, I should have manifested an incredible life of mental, emotional, spiritual and material abundance by now.

You don't see your life as abundant?

Of course I'm abundant in many ways. I don't mean to sound ungrateful but—

God forbid.

I guess I don't feel fulfilled because I still haven't achieved the goals I set myself. I see other people manifest what they want in their lives. Why haven't I been able to achieve the same thing? It's not as if I've sat back and waited for it to drop into my lap! I've created countless opportunities where the universe could have stepped in and given me a helping hand.

I've often tried to connect with—

I remember one time some years back when my wife and I focused very hard on creating the opportunity to purchase a property that was going to be auctioned. We meditated on it three times a day for weeks. I practiced every manifestation technique I knew. I even had dreams about living in it and walking through the rooms. I took that as a very positive sign.

Then one morning as I was waking and still in the *in-between* state, I started my visualization process. Do you know what happened next? Just as I was seeing myself walking through the front door of the property a voice in my head said—

It is not in the co-creator's best interest.

Exactly! I sprung up in bed, wide eyed, unable to comprehend—
It was *you*?

It was *me*.

Well, thank you very much! I thought I was losing my mind. I'd never used the term "co-creator" so I knew something was going on. Why didn't you explain? Why didn't you keep talking to me?

I did keep talking, but you weren't in the mood to listen. You were so preoccupied with your own tantrum that you couldn't hear me.

11

What did you mean by "it wasn't in my best interest"?

It wasn't your time. But I'm now here to tell you that it is your time—to move beyond the "poor me" reruns groove and own the responsibility of the powerful co-creator that you truly are.

That's a bit harsh! I do have feelings you know. Where's your compassion?

Having emotions and "emotionalizing" are two very different and distinctly opposing psychological manifestos—the reaction of which you just displayed, a perfect example.

I never said I'd perfected it.

A person in their truth uses their emotions as a guidance system to help them gauge how they truly feel about something, to help them stay centered and in alignment with their higher self. Using your emotions to manipulate, to "emotionalize" a situation so that you feel a sense of justification, is the reverse, because it can only ever satisfy the shadow self, the negative ego.

The whole point is that I *was* trying to manifest my co-creative powers. But it's as if something always gets in my way. What is it with this sense I have of being hemmed in by a "restriction grid"?

Your *perceived* "restriction grid" is merely your frustration of wanting to jump off the precipice before you have remembered how to use your wings. In your psyche you've always known that your chance to fly was coming, but if you'd leapt off the edge too soon it would be like jumping into the void with a parachute; your opportunity to soar to the heights of your highest potential would have been limited to a short lived hover followed by a sure and sudden descent.

But why wasn't it in my best interest to manifest a bit of abundance and achievement in the meantime? What harm could it have done?

In your particular case, you decided it would have been too high a risk as it may have taken you off on another path, steering you in a direction other than the one you planned before your incarnation.

I used to believe in all that, but I'm not sure I do anymore.

You see, as it is for many pioneering souls of your ilk, the timing for achieving your true mission was never set in concrete; it has always been an absolute variable, dependent on many other factors that would bring your mission's purpose to a synchronized timing so as to fit in with the bigger picture of what you and souls of your lineage are here to do. It is your impatience of living for the *future dream* and not being present in the *now moment* that has brought you to the point where you are.

What point?

The point where you've allowed yourself to become so angry and frustrated that you believe God has forsaken you.

I don't blame God or anyone else for that matter for my disappointments!

OK.

I do not! I've always believed and owned the fact that I'm the creator of my own reality. You have to give me that!

Are you saying that your bouts of screaming and cursing God all those times was just my imagination?

OK! So I lost the plot a few times. I've reached the end of my tether. I'm just trying to figure out why I keep recreating more of the same. And I'm sure that most people on the planet would relate to what I'm saying.

An empowered co-creator stays centered in the knowledge that they are here to enjoy what the world has to offer and that their life will unfold as was intended. If you held this as your focus, nothing would faze you.

Oh, so much easier said than done! Particularly from where you're standing... hovering, whatever! I've obviously not reached that level.

Oh, so much easier denied than embraced! Particularly from where your current mind-set—*set* being the operative word—is currently at. You've simply allowed your shadow to stop you from piercing the veil.

Shadow! What shadow?

In good time. Let us go over the questions in your journaling exorcise.

You mean, "exercise".

In the beginning "there was the word". Believe me, I was there, and I don't misuse them. In your journaling you were in the process of "exorcising" your demons, your fears. Shall we proceed?

I'm all-ears.

In relation to your *perceived* failure, your *delayed* success will be your saving grace. Your philosophy does not work *for* you—*you* must work for your philosophy—remembering that *beliefs* get in your way, but *ideas* are ever expansive. In the bigger picture there are no wrongs, just choices.

Yeah, yeah, yeah! I've heard it all before. So what about karma? For years, all the books and channels have preached and explained the purpose of karma, but now the latest catchcry is that there's no such thing as karma! And apparently this information-of-opposites is claimed to have come from the same "inspired" guidance! How exactly does that make any sense?

Because the concept of "karma" is just that—a *conceptualized system of beliefs*.

I thought it was universal law.

The philosophy of karma has been created and *actualized* by a *belief system*.

So it's not real?

16

Not in the true sense of word *real*.

What do you mean?

Humanity's underlying beliefs has nearly always been in a reward-if-you're-good and a punishment-if-you're-bad system—in truth a belief in martyrdom—that wants you to accept that you are here under the pretext of punishment and retribution. Therefore, under such a system, if you were to make a conscious decision to take an action with negative intention, be it in this life or from a past incarnation, it would eventually be returned or reflected as a *re-action*, which you call "bad karma".

That's because the word "karma" congers up the idea of punishment-for-wrongdoing. Anyway, I think it's just the universe wanting revenge.

"Revenge" is an emotionalized human concept. And that's because what you term karma comes from a negative emotional standpoint, and is usually misinterpreted as "punishment". In truth it is simply a program created by humanity's belief in *"An eye for an eye and a tooth for a tooth"* attitude.

As described in some Western scriptures, *"As ye sow, so shall ye also reap"* is closer to capturing the essence of universal law and its functioning. When you plant a seed, whether good or bad, if you continue to energize and feed it with intention

and belief, it will bear the fruit of your attention—
because you create and manifest your own reality.
In fact, as you have heard before, the universe will
rearrange itself to accommodate your *perceived*
picture of reality.

So what are you saying, there's really no such
thing as karma?

The concept and cycle of "karma" can only exist
as part of the *manifestation program* so to speak,
as long as it is perpetuated through a system of
believing *in it*. It was not intended by any great-
being-in-the-sky that you live under this pretext. It
is a manifesto devised by and actualized by the
very co-creators that continue to support the karmic
program by feeding it the energy source of *belief*. If
you don't feed it, it dies.

The results derived from such a system are
merely the universe mirroring what you project
outward. Once this principle is fully understood and
embraced, you will realize that hurting another, is as
a matter of fact, hurting yourself and vice versa.

The concept of karma has generally been viewed
in a negative light, because it is mostly recognized
as a universal balancing tool for the disproportionate
use and abuse of energy—

I'll tell you about disproportionate use and abuse of
energy! Clearly I should have followed the instructions

on that banner in orbit on approach for my current incarnation! "If you want to succeed on this plane of existence, don't bother landing unless you're willing to use, abuse, lie, cheat and deceive your way in and out of any situation you find yourself in! Oh! And let's not forget, trample, crush and pulverize your opponents— sometimes friends if need be—into the mud of betrayal while climbing up the ladder to fulfill your desire for success, power and control. These are the only true and tried tactics suggested for self-preservation on this third lump of clay from the sun, because this dimension is a place of *survival of the fittest*—or more appropriately described, *survival of the most cunning.*"

I'm sorry; did I go off on a tangent?

—However, the Eastern philosophers of karma also wanted you to believe that if you take an action with a positive intention this will be met with a karmic *response* of the same, so that you would behave in a manner that was in keeping with their teachings. The only difference between their teachings and that of the Christian faith, is that you got more than one lifetime to get it right; instead of going to hell as punishment after one life of being *naughty*, you would instead relive a life of punishment where you would experience being the *inflicted* instead of the *inflictor*—

Did you just ignore me?

—Hence, "karma" is simply a word, a word that has in recent times been emotionalized to infer punishment more than reward, rather than it's true state of *neutrality*, until, of course, it is fed and in turn activated by the energy of *belief*—

OK! I can play this game... and further more, in small print you'll find listed on the bottom of the banner: "If you do not employ these survival skills you will most likely be condemned to a life of mental, emotional and physical pain, suffering and dissatisfaction, and let's not forget disease, while being used and abused by a system set up to restrict you at every turn until you can bear it no more. At this point you can choose to go into denial and live out a life of mediocrity, deaden all your faculties and senses with a diversity of mind-dulling vices such as alcohol, smoking or recreational drugs that are readily available in a variety of strengths to suit your desired length of get-me-the-hell-off-this-planet doses."

—And in final analysis; as long as you continue to believe in and energize these concepts, in one way or another, it will in like continue to serve your self fulfilling prophecy—perpetuating your Victim and Victimizer mentality—until you are ready to transform these systems of beliefs to a true state of *knowingness* that the only important moment is in the present, in turn raising your awareness to a

level that will move you beyond the old program of
Keeping **A** **R**edundant **M**indset **A**ctualized.

Is that what KARMA stands for?

It may as well.

So, are you saying that karma only exists as long
as we believe we're here under a *Reward and
Punishment* system for deeds done?

Allow me to ponder this... yes; I am almost
certain that is what I have been trying to get across
during the last few minutes. Besides, why would
you want to believe in and support such a concept
when, as you yourself often state, *"You'd better
watch out because karma can be a real mother f—"*

Stop! It's not appropriate for you to make state-
ments like that here!

I am not making a statement; I am merely
paraphrasing and suggesting that you, as you
yourself often state, are a BC... blunt rhyming
with...

OMG! Stop it! This just isn't right. You can't
talk like that! Besides, you're portraying me as
though I'm—

21

Sometimes a man of double standards, perhaps even hypocrisy? God forbid! Do you seriously think philosophers and avatars of the past didn't use the *colorful* language-of-the-time to express themselves?

You mean… they cursed? That's blasphemy!

Oh ye Gods!

There's more than one?

It is my intention to open your mind to the next stage of your evolution. This is what the new writings and information are putting forward into the mass-conscious soup of possibilities; that it is time to move beyond the perpetuation game and become all that you can be *now*—not by some reward or punishment system where you reap the consequences of your actions at a later time. Such a system is a double-edged sword, because your belief in it creates the actual opportunity and circumstance for the manifestation of the *Victim and Victimizer* role, which then has to be enacted by the souls—the players—who created it in the first place to fulfill and play out the energetic cycle of intention that was set in motion.

The KARMA *program* is old and outdated. If you relinquish this program, this system of beliefs, there will be no need for the *Victim and Victimizer* roles, because the circumstance will never be actualized or made manifest.

It is time for an upgrade; to keep pace with the times because as you have become aware, your experience of time is changing, time is speeding up, as humanity approaches the next stage of its evolution.

Whose idea was the concept of evolution anyway? What a slow and torturous way to evolve.

Only because humanity chooses to travel the unconscious path of the *treadmill*, has it been what you might call an arduous process of *Evolution-by-Default*. Now, due to so many people looking for new answers, there has been a dislodging of people's *beliefs,* as they are replacing this with the expansiveness of ever-changing *ideas*, evolving exponentially through the more enlightened process of *Evolution-by-Conscious-Choosing*.

So is that what's meant by those who say karma is finished? That we can *choose* to move on from it?

Indeed. Let us now move on to your concept of a curse as listed in your blurb to the universe. You cannot be cursed unless there is a part of you that is open to its influence. This can also be connected to your karmic—if you choose to stay connected to that program—past-life ties with the person who is putting out that intention. You could not attract it vibrationally unless you match its frequency through your intention, beliefs and attitudes about yourself, which in turn activates *the law of attraction*. A curse is merely an energy-grid of *intention* that someone tries to place on you, like a virus entering your system. You can neutralize its effect by changing your attitude and belief system about such matters. The native tribesman only falls dead with the pointing-of-the-bone by the witch doctor because it has been instilled in him since birth, ingrained in every cell and fiber of his being by a powerful belief system, that that is what will happen. It is simply a fear-induced programming of his cells that says, if the bone is ever pointed at you every function in your vehicle will shut down—as in *instant death*.

"Intention" is a very powerful tool of manifestation. Your positive emotions of compassion, happiness and goodwill will generate what you would call "preferred outcomes", where as negative emotions of anger and bitterness—laced with a touch of your cynicism—particularly if repressed or perpetuated, is a highly and proven means of allowing the manifestation of negative outcomes and even for disease to eventually cripple or terminate your physical vehicle, often faster than you can revoke such negative programming. This method has a far greater ratio of success than any of your mind-altering substances. Your sciences are now beginning to grasp and acknowledge the truth of the fact that the state of your emotions has a great bearing on your health and wellbeing.

Just what are you suggesting? That if I don't change my attitude I could become cynical?

Become? Are you familiar with the phrase *"definition of..."*?

You know, for a *Being* pretending to be from higher realms, you are incredibly rude.

Only from your current standpoint and what you consider an acceptable standard of decency. Besides, I don't recall at any time indicating that I was *"holier than thou"*!

So, whoever or whatever you are, why has there been such a long delay in my being able to manifest my hopes, dreams and wishes? I've clearly been working from the old outdated program, so is it the result of a "karmic" *re-action* to my past actions?
And no flowery responses! A "Yes" or a "No" will do.

Yes—

That clears that up.

—And no.

It is a dichotomy. Your perceived delay is partly because of a karmic *re-action*, and partly because of a karmic *response*.

So, because I've intentionally done some bad things, but I've also intentionally done some good things—and let's not forget that I've held on to the belief in a victim and victimizer philosophy and for the greater part still do—I'm in the process of reaping the results of both?

You want to turn it into an emotional issue of good or bad, wrong or right, but you must keep in mind, in the bigger picture it is simply about the process of making choices through experience. From this perspective there is no judgment made through the process of your favorite pastime of *emotionalization*! It is merely the process of universal law fulfilling what you believe.

But why is it so damned hard? Why am I finding it such a challenge? Why the hell can't I break free from of it?

Your circumstance is that you've allowed the distractions of life to blur your vision of where you know you are truly headed.

But I don't know where I'm headed anymore. And I'm aware of a fear building. I fear that I might have missed the boat this lifetime. I'm aware of a sense of bitterness creeping in to my every thought.

Yet another dichotomy—you are partly feeling fear because the thing you've been waiting for is soon about to manifest in your life.

Oh please! Not another fortuitous prediction telling me of the wonders that lay on the path ahead of me. It's all beginning to wear just a little thin.

There is an aspect of you that has become so addicted to the living-for-the-dream syndrome, that instead of staying centered in and enjoying the *now moment*, you are afraid to move out of the *comfort zone* that you've become so used to.

Believe me mental torture and emotional frustrations are not states I would call comfortable.

I also believe you are familiar with the term "self inflicted"?

Hey! You've got no right to—

When your dream comes knocking at your door and you find yourself standing face to face with it, you go into panic because you have to turn-the-page of your "story" and move beyond the limitation and sum of what you think you know. Many choose to stay on the same page all their lives. Is that also your intention?

—

Hello, is anyone there?

—

Now that you are getting closer to tackling your major life's mission, you are feeling a resistance.

Resistance? Resistance to what?

To fulfill your agreement and what it entails.

What agreement?

To dispel a myth.

What myth?

We're getting to that. But first we need to set the parameters and establish your perception of who you think I am.

Two

You're probably just a figment of my imagination.

Your imagination is the only faculty through
which I can reach you. Your imagination is your
way to reach beyond the constraints of linear time.
Imagination is what has created all the technological
wonders of your lifestyle.
Imagination is the process that sustains *Creation*.
Imagination—

All right! I get the picture. Well, if you're using
my mind to communicate with me, I command that
you show yourself through my imagination. Show
me a vision of yourself—show me something grand!

Interesting choice of words. However, since it is
your wish that is *my* command...

You really are quite funny. Sure you're not the
spirit of some deceased comedian?

The universe is filled with humor. For your first task I ask you to go outside and look up to the sky.

—

How'd you go?

It's a lovely clear star-studded night, but I couldn't see anything.

You didn't look *between* the stars. Go take another look.

—

Did you look closely?

Yes, I gazed up to the cosmos and it's very dark. And no, there were no spaceships, no satellites, not even a plane. What if you're just some kind of extraterrestrial creature with telepathic powers and a warped sense of humor?

What did you see *between* the stars?

There's *nothing* between the stars except black space.

Exactly.

Are we having some kind of communication problem here?

You asked to see something grand, something of myself.

Empty space is the grandest thing you could come up with?

What you refer to as being *nothing* is the most abundant and active source in the universe.

How can the blackness of space be active if it's empty?

That is what science had concluded until recently. It has since been discovered that the *nothingness* that you can't see makes up more than 90 percent of the entire universe. Now that's *grand*! And that *something* is called "dark matter".

And so what does that have to do with you? I expected to see a flying angel spotlighted in brilliant white.

Now you're getting warm.

You're an angel!

Thank you.

No, I mean, are you an angel?

For the purpose of this exchange—in a manner of speaking—we could say that—

Here we go with the cryptic stuff again. Either you are or you're not.

Your perception of "Angel" would at this time best help you grasp the overall picture of where we are headed.

I get it! You're an *archangel*.

I have been called that in certain scriptures.

I knew it! Like John Travolta in the movie *Michael*. You've been sent down to Earth on a mission and you've chosen me to help you.

You're very good at bringing the conversation back to yourself.

No, no, no. I'm totally getting it. I'm at your service. You can show yourself now. Do your stuff. Flap your wings. Do whatever it takes. Make me smell those chocolate-chip cookies—

I'm not that kind of angel.

You really are funny! How much time have we got? Have your feathers started falling out yet?

Listen up! I'm not making your incredibly active imagination wrong—though verging on the side of *overactive*—but I'd appreciate it if you could tone it down a little. You will need to call on all your reasoning and coping mechanisms once you understand who I truly am.

Then show yourself. Manifest in front of me in a tangible form and everything will be made clear.

Yes it would, but no, not yet.

Why not?

Because, with your current understanding and conditioning, once you learn with *whom* you are dealing, your perception of me would cause you to see a vision that may not be pleasing to you.

I don't get it.

You will.

If you're not feeling well because your days here on earth are coming to an end, I can deal with that. I can understand it if you think a bald-winged angel isn't so hip!

—

OK. So, we agree that you are an archangel. Which one? Michael?

No.

Gabriel?

No.

Raphael?

No.

Archangel Uriel?

No.

Ariel? Azrael? Raguel?

—

Got it! You're Archangel Metatron, the head of all archangels. The archangel that speaks to Carlos Santana in his dreams and helps him to write his music.

No.

They're all the main ones I remember from Sunday school. I don't know much about other archangels.

Yes you do.

I do?

Your concept of an archangel is a metaphor that was created by early theologians as a simplified way of trying to explain spiritual hierarchy and levels of consciousness within *Creation*. In reality, there are countless levels of beings that play many roles in the governing of spiritual and physical realms.

That doesn't answer who you are. Are you one of the archangels that we haven't heard about?

You can rest assured that the entire world knows about me. I am the most well-known and well-remembered archangel of them all. For my name and my deeds have been used in vain for centuries.

Can your give me some kind of hint.

I just did.

OK. So I'm a bit slow on the pickup.

Yes, I noticed. Just remember, you asked for this. Allow me to embrace you...

Embrace me? I just want a vision that'll clear up who I'm conversing with. Hang on. The lights are dimming. No, my sight is going... it's as if a veil's being drawn across my line of vision. What the hell... I'm going blind! What's happening?

Do you remember?

This happened once years ago while I was using a meditation technique with a group of people, where we stared at a candle flame. It was a bit of a dichotomy really.

"Dichotomy" is my middle name.

Really?

No, but it could be.

Oh, I see. It's that universal humor again. Anyway, as I gazed at the flame my vision began to fade to blackness. I was too scared to let myself go into it.

I know, but there was another time.

That's right! When I was in my early teens, I'd been left alone in the dentist's chair after having laughing gas, waiting for the effects of the needle to set in. I remember closing my eyes. When I opened them I panicked because it was pitch black in the room, even though the sun had been streaming through the window only moments before. I wondered what had happened. I didn't want to embarrass myself, so—

You closed and opened your eyes widely several times, but your vision remained the same. You sat back in the chair and prayed that your sight be restored.

The gas had the effect of momentarily lowering your barriers, but when I realized that you weren't hearing me, I released you from my embrace, which also restored your sight. The dentist returned and you asked him if the laughing gas could have the effect of blocking your vision. When you explained what had taken place, he looked at you as though you were making it up.

Oh my God! I just had a very dark and scary thought.

Now, as your primal fear that is connected to the mass-conscious memory bank of humanity, makes its way from your subconscious to your conscious mind, I will release you from my embrace once more. I ask that you do not judge this experience hastily before you are given clarity.

Oh shit! There's only one other archangel from the Bible that I can remember—one of the two that sat at the side of God—the one that fell from grace and was banished from heaven to become ruler of hell and the sinners of earth.

Oh dear God! I ask my guides and Angels of light to protect me from this demon embracing me with his shroud of darkness. I consider myself a spiritual person rather than religious but I now recite in the name of the Father and the Holy Ghost:

OUR FATHER, WHO ART IN HEAVEN, HALLOWED BE THY NAME.

Thy kingdom come.

Thy will be done, On earth as it is in heaven.

Give us this day our daily bread.

And forgive us our trespasses,

As we forgive those who trespass against us.

And lead us not into temptation,

But deliver us from evil.

For thine is the kingdom,

and the power,

and the glory,

for ever and ever.

Amen.

I ask that the angels of light send away all negative spirits.

—

Anyone there?

    Just me. An inspiring prayer, don't you think? Too bad there is no hell, nor no evil, at least in the context that you have just used.

The Lord is my Shepherd;
I shall not want.
He maketh me to lie down
In green pastures;
He leadeth me
Beside the still waters;
He restoreth my soul;
He leadeth me in the paths
Of righteousness for His Name's sake.
Yea, though I walk through the valley
Of the shadow of death,
I will fear no evil...
BE GONE ALL EVIL SPIRITS!

—

    Not bad considering you haven't been to Sunday school since your were eight years old. A slight overreaction in my opinion, however your power of prayer has worked well. All entities with negative intention have moved away.

Which archangel are you?

You have already worked out my *archetype*. Move beyond your fear and say it.

Oh my God!

In a manner of speaking—

You're Lucifer! The fallen angel!

You know, for someone who dislikes so immensely being cut across mid-sentence—

What!

I have been called by many names over the eons, but fallen I am not.

How does that explain the theological description of who you are?

Man's descriptions are all too often tainted with his limited vision, perceived through fear-colored lenses.

Well, shouldn't the most powerful archangel who sits at the side of God and then forsakes him be feared?

It is not I who should be feared, but the *fear* that resides in the hearts of men.

What do you mean?

First let us clear up the issue of who you think I am. In some of your religious scriptures I have been described as the Archangel Lucifer who has forsaken God. This is one of the greatest misconceptions of Western religion.

Oh really!

In relation to the "fallen archangel" scenario created by the early Christian theologians, the clue that would unravel their intention to demonize my true nature is contained in the Latin term "lucem ferre".

How's that?

The name Lucifer is actually derived from the term "lucem ferre" which means *bringer* or *bearer of light*. This was originally applied to the *morning star* Venus, which was one of the many ancient names that venerated her shimmering beauty as she would herald each new dawn. The Greeks adopted this term and translated it to "phos-phoros" meaning *light bearer*. "Lucifer" was also the name given to the *morning star* in Roman astronomy.

41

But how can you explain away what happened? How did we come to think of Lucifer as the ruler of hell and the sinners on Earth?

Somewhere along the line the relatively modern Christian theologians chose to misinterpret the meaning of the word so that it conjured up all kinds of fear for the religious minded.

An ancient theological terror campaign!

In simple terms, when theologians decided they needed to create a central character to *place blame* on and at the same time find a way to demonize the pagan beliefs of the past, they chose to borrow from the ancient Egyptians. Particular attention was given to their canine God Seth, which inspired them to conjure up the demonic character that later became known as Satan, first to blame for the hardship of life on earth and secondly to vilify a God that had been revered in ancient spiritual practice.

We need someone to blame, someone to take responsibility for our hardship. Why not the angel that had forsaken God?

The story about a vengeful God and an evil fallen archangel who had forsaken him is fictitious. Yet, because it generated much fear it gave the

Church control over the populace with a new set of
rules relating to the new Christian doctrine of God
and how to worship *him*.

They just made it up to suit their own ends? Any
of them incarnate as politicians recently?

Let us say they found the perfect opportunity
through the concept of *Lucem Ferre* to fulfill their
needs.

I suppose it's common knowledge now that the
Bible has been rewritten and reinterpreted many times
over the centuries.

In this case they plagiarize part of an original
Hebrew text, the Old Testament book of Isaiah
14:12, which speaks about a fallen Babylonian
king: "How art thou fallen from heaven, O Lucifer,
son of the morning! How art thou cut down to the
ground, which didst weaken the nations!"
This was merely Isaiah using the shimmering
morning star Venus as metaphor for the fading light
of a once powerful Babylonian king.
The Christian scribes who translated the scriptures into the Church's Latin tongue at that time,
seized the opportunity and changed the story of the
fallen Babylonian monarch into the tale of a fallen
archangel.

Have to give full points for imagination. Seems the Church invented the first master's degree in manipulation and falsification.

The theologians gave this new character the name Lucifer, which served the double purpose of demonizing the Luciferian philosophy, a philosophy practiced by many who believed that there were avatars sent to earth whom were *Bringers or Bearers of Light*.

According to the Church, once Lucifer had been banished from heaven he fell from grace and became ruler over the demons of hell and the sinners of earth. This new doctrine successfully instilled enough fear and trepidation into their followers, allowing for easy manipulation and swaying them into believing that the only way to redemption was through the Church.

So there was never mention of a satanic character in the earlier scriptures?

That hideous creation and hellish nightmare was never part of the original Hebrew Scriptures. Even today, the Jewish faith and others have no place for the concept of hell or a satanic ruler. The entire story was created to generate fear in the populace so that the word of the Western Church would reign supreme and remain sacrosanct and unchallenged.

Did anyone outside the Church know what had been done?

Many ancient religious and esoteric groups were aware of what was taking place and had to go underground for fear of being persecuted. Any persons or groups that were labelled *freethinkers* at that time of history were mercilessly hunted down and silenced.

They were followers of Lucifer. Doesn't that mean they were worshippers of Satan?

Over time the story of the fallen archangel did evolve into the concept of Satan the Prince of Darkness, but as you will learn these references stand for very different things.

The followers of Lucifer considered themselves "Luciferian" in nature, but in the true translation of the word. These souls were merely seeking to attain higher truths and consciousness through the "Luciferian Path", the path of en*light*enment, much like the New Age or Mind, Body and Spirit movement of current times. This is an extraordinary religious irony—they were searching for the *bearer of light* within themselves, which is the exact opposite of the Church's labeling of their aspirations as satanic or evil. Many sects also used the name "Lucifer" as a surname for *Goddesses of light*, such as Artemis, Aurora, and Hecate.

The Luciferians also presented another problem for the Church—a problem they considered an extremely dangerous threat to their authority. Because they were looking for the *light of God and truth* within themselves Luciferians had no need for the external structure or dogma of the Church. That was something the Church was powerless to stop and considered intolerable.

So that's why they named the fallen archangel, Lucifer, so as to demonize the philosophy of Luciferians. They didn't want anyone to champion the torch of truth and light because it would challenge their authority.

Yes, however the concept of the *fallen archangel* scenario was also made up. All freethinkers were considered enemies of the Church's patriarchal authority.

What an incredible story.

Quite frankly, even if I had an evil bone in my Beingness, I couldn't possibly have made this scenario any more melodramatic if I'd tried! Only a blend of human consciousness combined with a touch of fear and ignorance could manage such a task.

The irony for modern-day theologians is that in early times Jesus Christ was also referred to as

Luciferian in the true sense of the word—*the light bearer* or *the bringer of light*. The term *child of light* and *shining one* has also been attributed to this term's meaning.

"Child of Light", as in baby Jesus?

In Revelation 22:16 Jesus refers to himself as the root and offspring of David and the bright *morning star (Venus)—Lucem Ferre*, "Lucifer".

The religious minded would consider everything you've said sacrilegious and abominable!

I cannot apologize for the manipulation and falsification of past documents. Anyone who is interested can research this for themselves.

So millions of people have lived in fear of a fictitious evil being for hundreds of years for nothing! It's all been a big take?

The concept of one *evil being* who is the ruler of Hell and the sinners on earth was intentionally fabricated. Christian scholars also went to Egypt long after the collapse of the Pharaohs rule, destroyed and defaced their temples and then plagiarized many of their religious teachings. Much of the later biblical rewrites are based on translations of the ancient Egyptian doctrines. If you

study the subject you will find astounding correl-
ations, particularly the similarity between Seth the
canine God of the underworld and the Western
concept of Satan—the ruler of Hell.

Next time you stand outside any of the older
style churches take a close look at their structure. If
you remove the walls in your mind's eye, the
layout, chambers, halls and cathedrals themselves
are very reminiscent of the ancient temples of
Egypt.

Where do you think the idea for referring to the
philosopher Jesus as the Son of God—God incarnate
in human form—came from?

You mean... they even plagiarized the same
religious practice of Egypt's Pharaoh as being representative of God incarnate?

The nerve! The hypocrisy! They destroy their
temples, defame their pagan ways, and then have the
audacity to use those very same principles in their
own writings and structures?

The ancient Egyptians were aware of my
existence and purpose, but they did not vilify my
presence by turning me into the shady character of
darkness and inflictor of pain and suffering as the
Christian theologians did. They simply accepted
that *darkness* is merely the balance of its opposite,
light.

What about their pagan ways of worshipping many different Gods? Isn't that against God's law?

As you believe, there are as many ways to knowing God as there are paths to the top of a mountain. Metaphorically speaking, choosing to worship many different aspects of the Deity rather than just one, is no more or less unrealistic than the image of a bearded patriarchal God sitting on his throne in heaven with countless angels and archangels administering his holy realm of Creation. It is merely a tangible image on which to focus your attention and prayers.

I've always been suspicious of that image.

The ancient Chinese philosophy also grasped the concept from a more balanced perspective when they introduced the principle of the Yin and the Yang. They understood that for *Creation* to be made manifest, there must be an equal balance between light and dark or the masculine and feminine—the fundamental law of polarity.

Part of the reason why the misguided Western theologians conjured up the concept of Hell as a place of pain and suffering, was because of a deep-seated memory of a time before their incarnation. It is a spiritual joke amongst souls who are waiting to incarnate back to earth.

What are you saying?

That the most common place to which you can incarnate for the opportunity to live a hellish life of mental, emotional and physical pain and suffering, is what humanity has set up on earth—as you can imagine, it was even more so back in those times.

Now who's sounding cynical?

Don't delude yourself. Have you read your history books or viewed your news broadcasts recently? They only touch the edge of the totality that is the truth. And even then it is stretched and manipulated to suit the trend and political agenda of the times.

You mentioned Jesus. I've often wondered what he and other avatars of the various faiths would say and do if they were able to stand on a podium and deliver a message to our religious and world leaders today.

The words will come.

Why did religion become devoid of sensitivity and so patriarchal in its attitude?

It was a reflection of the times and the mass-conscious belief system. The new Christian religion deemed that there was no longer a place for the sensitivities of the heart in religious practice. The Church set out to suppress the feminine principle as the new patriarchal order excluded women and the symbolic Goddess of matriarchy.

You're a feminist?

The patriarchal biblical God was to be feared and venerated as a male God of judgment and retribution. There was no allowance for the balanced perspective of masculine and feminine in this concept. The Church relied on these *fear tactics* as a political means of controlling the people.

Nothing's changed much. Fear is still the driving force behind any political agenda these days.

Hence, as man disconnected his mind from his heart, the quest for the Holy Grail became a symbolic gesture for the external search to find the matriarchal principle he had in fact himself rejected. But of course, the outer search would be eternally in vain, for the Holy Grail was always just within his reach, if only he'd looked within and opened his heart.

The Grail is a symbol of the heart?

It is a symbol of the heart and mind united in balance.

51

How could the Church have got it so wrong?

In the bigger picture there are no wrongs, there are just choices of experiences. We will go into more detail about the lesson of *choices* in another segment. I did converse with some of the theologians of the past. I was trying to help them understand the metaphysical principles of *Polarity* that governs the spiritual technology behind *Creation*.

You spoke to them?

They were very receptive to visions and interpreting dreams in earlier times. But because of their misunderstanding of the Dark Forces, fear took hold and instead of accepting the true principles of *Creation*, they took my teachings and turned them in to something fearful and negative.

However, earlier Bible writers didn't even believe in or teach any kind of doctrine that included the concept of Satan. It did not even enter their consciousness.

I've also heard that there are many missing doctrines that have been removed over time—doctrines that spoke of the purpose and principle behind the philosophy of reincarnation and many others relating to women and the principles of matriarchy.

This took place when *Emperor Constantine the Great* called the *Council of Nicea* in AD 325. Several hundred religious leaders came together and voted to remove many biblical writings by those who were considered to be of questionable origin. Particularly those writings that were complimentary to the matriarchal principles of *Creation*. The writings on reincarnation were specifically deleted so that people would think they only had one chance, one lifetime to achieve entry into heaven. This greatly increased the psychological stronghold of the Church over their parishioners as they clambered at its door to give away their power.

During the centuries that followed all kinds of writings were added to *thicken the plot*, so to speak. In light of this I am going to give you another version of what you know as the "Fall from Grace". And herein lies the answer to your mission.

And that is?

To record our dialogue.

Oh, so I can listen back to it?

Not that kind of recording.

What other type of recording is there.

The old fashioned way—ink and paper.

You want me to print this out so I can re-read it?

Yes... but also so others can read it.

You mean you want this published? You want *me* to admit to the world that I've had a personal and intimate conversation with an archangel? Oh, and not just any old archangel folks—we're talking Lucifer! The ruler of darkness, the one you know as inflictor of pain and suffering. And guess what? *He* wants to give *you* a message through *me*!

You catch on fast. And further more, this dialogue is to dispel a myth.

Finally, the *myth* thing!

The myth that *Light is good* and representative of a benevolent God in heaven, and that *Dark is bad* and representative of Lucifer, a malevolent ruler of hell and the sinners on earth. For in fact, the Forces of Light and the Forces of Darkness are each the equal half of the one and same Divinity.

Are you stark raving mad! So you not only want an open declaration to the world in black and white that states that I willingly had a conversation with Lucifer, but a declaration that suggests that the dark forces of the universe are one and the same with God! Add to that, a few paragraphs back you suggested

54

that in ancient times Jesus' nickname was Lucifer! Do you know what this will do to me? Can you even begin to imagine the repercussions?

I think *I* would have some idea. But humanity doesn't live in the "dark ages" anymore.

I take it you're speaking metaphorically?

Indeed! I am referring to the "dark ages" as the time when most of humanity chose to remain "unconscious" by hiding their awareness in the darkness of subconscious obscurity. Thinking too deeply was a dangerous pastime back then.

But nowadays people want their "awareness" to be brought out into the light; they want to become conscious, to create a New Age of en*light*enment. That is why there has been such an explosion of information available about spirituality through the New Awareness movement. You truly are entering a New Age of accepting what has been known and documented through many of the great cultures for millennia.

But I could be the brunt of attacks from people everywhere who will think I'm Satan's right hand man. If I were in the wrong century, I'd be burned at the stake. Why have you chosen me to be your sacrificial lamb? Who am I anyway? Why don't you

contact the Pope or, better still, some renegade theologian who wants to rectify the mistakes of the past?

I have.

You have *what*?

I have contacted a renegade theologian who
wants to rectify his fear-induced choices of his past.

Where are you going with this?

You were there.

Oh, of course I was—I was where?

In a past incarnation, you were involved with
defaming my name. You helped to steal and plagiarize teachings from cultures that you considered to be
primitive heathens. You helped the Church of ancient times gain control and force their beliefs on
others. Why do you think you have such feelings of
disapproval for the Church this time round?

—

Anyone there?

I was there? I helped to set up the whole thing!

56

As you said earlier, "The nerve! The hypocrisy!" Yes, you helped destroy the temples and defame the pagan ways of people you once considered heathens. And you then helped to integrate many of those very same principles into the writings of Christianity.

No please... not Egypt. I love Egypt! I totally resonate with the beauty and simplicity of their lifestyle and intricacies of their ancient religion.

This lifetime you do. But back in that incarnation, during the rise of the Christian faith you considered their pagan ways primitive and barbaric. Quite a dichotomy, don't you think?

Are you screwing with my mind?

No.

This is terrible.

That I'm not?

I feel so bad.

I feel the onset of another overdramatised Shakespearean moment.

I feel I should apologize to you.

You did.

I did?

The moment you died. But you have one saving grace.

And that is?

In your heart, you believed you were doing the right thing.

But I was doing the wrong thing.

Expressing your belief as an idea is not wrong, but making someone else's wrong and enforcing your will against another is certainly not in the best interest of—and only serves to hinder their and your spiritual—evolution. The flipside of this type of circumstance is where the role of the "inflictor" is in fact fulfilling the need of the "inflicted".

What?

This phenomenon could easily be called the *law of metaphysical collusion*, serving to perpetuate and fulfill the requirement of each player's need of KARMA. We will delve more into this later.

Please tell me I've also lived a life where I stood for the truth?

You have also lived a life where you stood for the truth.

Really?

Many times. But standing up for your truth and freethinking ways was often met with a touch of resistance.

I was punished?

You were burned at the stake.

Oh please! That's a typical New Age cliché! Everyone's either been burned at the stake, suffered at the hands of the Inquisition, or at the other end of the scale, held high-powered titles of priests, monarchs and other fanciful positions.

Indeed, as have you—experienced the extremes at both ends of the social scale and everything in-between. Why do you think so many people believe they were burned at the stake?

Because they're all a pack of drama queens! They'd rather not remember the ordinary and uneventful lives they lived.

Maybe so, but it's mainly because during a period that lasted over several centuries, millions of people who were suspected of practicing anything remotely pagan or esoteric were systematically hunted down, often tortured and then burned at the stake.

Millions?

Millions. Suddenly the term "cliché" doesn't fit so well in this scenario.

I knew someone once who thought he was the embodiment of Jesus incarnate. And he couldn't wait till he lit up and reignited his Christhood so that he could tell the world that Jesus was gay! They're the kind of *nutters* that give the New Age or Mind, Body and Spirit movement a bad name.

He was right—

I'm beginning to worry about your dark humor.

—about one thing.

What could he possibly have been right about?

That you are here to learn how to reignite your own Christhood. That has always been the central theme of all avatars' teachings, no matter what religion plagiarized their teachings.

What exactly are you getting at?

Jesus, Buddha, Krishna, Muhammad and many others were prophets and philosophers of their time. Through their intense search and final *allowing*, they awoke to a higher state of consciousness and embodied a universal truth. They became avatars, *Bearers of Light* in their own right and chose to share what they had discovered with their fellow seekers of truth, inspired and expressed from within their individual cultural influences.

What about the "Christhood" thing.

Everyone that comes to experience life on this planet has the potential to become Christed, to raise her or his awareness to a level of Christ Consciousness, or for that matter Buddha, Krishna or Muhammad Consciousness—it's all the same thing—to embody her or his higher angelic self—to bring back the balance—to become *Bearers of Light* in your own right. In short, to become enlightened. That has been the message of all the avatars throughout the ages.

"Angelic"? What's that got to do with anything?

It is symbolic of your higher nature. If you could see the energy-fields I see when I look at you from this side, your description would resemble something in the vein of what you term an angel.

Anyway, what's *Christ Consciousness* and becoming enlightened got to do with me? I haven't had any kind of awakening! I'm just a disillusioned soul lost on his path, wondering what it's all about like most of the rest of the world. For all the seeking I've done over the years, I haven't discovered any solutions. I don't want to go out there pretending to have answers. You've just finished telling me that I already tried that once. It didn't work! Remember?

Your experience from that life is why you hold such fear about your mission this time round. But what you must remember is that you volunteered for the job.

That's just it! I *don't* remember! I bet it's more like the Spiritual Hierarchy drafted me against my will.

You'll have to take my word for it.

And I suppose you spoke to me in that century as well. Is it any wonder I was turned into a roast! No doubt I was evangelizing stuff about how wonderful Lucifer was, even back then. *I* would have had *me* burned at the stake too if I'd heard such talk.

Your roasting in England was because you practiced spiritual beliefs that revered an all-encompassing God of love, peace, tolerance and harmony.

Oh! I see.

However, juxtaposition to this, you did also play the role of aggressor in another lifetime, but that was during the Spanish Inquisition. And I must say, you played that particular role spookily well.

Role?

In life you always choose to play out roles. Some come back to play out specific roles that set an example for the rest of the world.

So, is what's happening to me now some kind of karmic punishment? I mean, "redistribution of energy abuse"?

Let us say it is more like your choice to balance the books. You agreed to come down here and set the record straight with those who are ready to listen.

Down here? As in, down from heaven?

63

As in down from higher realms—realms that exist at *higher frequencies* of the consciousness scale.

But I don't remember agreeing to this.

You have been told about it before.

I have?

Remember the reading your had from a clair-voyant in 1986?

Yes.

What was it that she told you that has puzzled you ever since?

She told me there was a shaft of light behind me and that I was going to write something that the world was not ready to hear at that time. I didn't understand what she meant because I was working on an idea for a novel.

And what was the message you got in 1994?

It was said that I would have a book published that would cause some controversy. That there would be many people who would like it, but there would also be those who would attack its content.

64

Well, that time has come. This is it! There are many people around the world that are now ready to hear the concepts that I am sharing through dialogue with you.

What if I don't want to do it?

During your meditations over the years, you have continued to ask that you be used as an ambassador of Spirit's message. If you didn't want it, you wouldn't be sitting here writing this now.

You've always considered yourself a bit of a renegade. Well, here's your opportunity. I am offering you to take hold of the ladle that will "stir the pot" of stagnation—the very thing you've wanted to do for lifetimes. Why would you take a back-seat now?

Because I thought we would utilize the medium of my voice, my *singing* voice and the writing of novels and movie-scripts to spread the message.

And so we will, once you have fulfilled your first priority.

I don't see the point in writing a controversial conversational piece like this through *me*, and particularly for the public to see. As you may have noticed, I don't have the right temperament. I'm far too blunt and disrespectful for protocol and political correctness.

The term "cynical" would also nicely round off your list of qualities. That is exactly why you are the right man. You will push the boundary. You will go where angels fear to tread. You will ask the hard questions—questions that others would like to ask, but are too afraid to, for fear of repercussion and how they may look to others.

Surely there couldn't possibly be anything else to add to what's already been said in other writings?

I will be the judge of that.

That's fine, but there are hundreds of books, CD's, DVD's, self-help seminars and workshops that have been made available during the last several decades, going on and on about all kinds of wonderful philosophical concepts, jargon and ideas to assist people on their journey.

And they all have and are serving their purpose—

I don't disagree with that but—

—and have paved the way in preparation for those who are now ready to hear what I have to say through you and others that have been waiting in the wings on the stage of life.

What do you mean?

All the books, movies and seminars relating to these subject matters have played a vital role in preparing the way for other pieces of the jigsaw to be revealed and set in place, just as this conversation— piece of the jigsaw—will be in preparation for another placement. They are incremental steps, circuit breakers.

Circuit breakers?

Pieces of code that break down and transmute the "resistance factor" within the mass-consciousness belief system.

Pieces of "code"! You're referring to books, movies and recordings as pieces of code?

I use this terminology merely as a way to explain that everything holds an energetic imprint of frequencies. We will delve into this in later discussions. If you could see it from my perspective, you would see that whether letters and words on a page, words and music on a CD or images and sound on a DVD or film, they are merely sets of frequencies that are combined to induce and activate certain responses.

But truly, how many times can the same thing be rehashed and told in a different way?

As many ways as there are souls on the planet—over 6.8 billion and increasing with each passing moment.

Three

There is an entire audience out there who will resonate with your experience and your particular interpretation of my words.

What do you mean "interpretation" of your words? Aren't I just clairaudient and writing down what I'm hearing... feeling?

I can only connect to you through your imagination, which is based on the composite of all that you are—your experiences, concepts, beliefs and ideas developed over many lifetimes.

How could I ever have imagined in my wildest dreams that I was going to end up being personal assistant to Lucifer, the ruler of darkness.

I have enough faith in you to communicate my transmissions into words. The question is, do you?

I was thinking more along the line that these writings would be for myself, like a private one-on-one psychotherapy session, only my practitioner happens to be an archangel, a fallen one at that—well, I know you're not, now—but other people may not believe it.

The payment for your Archatherapy sessions will be to share them with others because they will find solace and insight through your journey, just as others will have their buttons pushed, possibly nudging them to look beyond their comfort zone and view things from a different perspective.

Yeah right! Even if it does get published, I'm sure your politically incorrect comments on sensitive religious issues will go down well with theologians and the Church. Besides, what publishing company is going to take on a writer who says he's been having a private conversation with *Lucifer* of all... people... Beings... whatever!

Where is your faith and belief in your co-creative powers?

As you know, they've been dormant for quite some time.

That was until we cleared many of your blockages.

We've cleared my blockages? I didn't feel a thing.

See how painless letting go of stagnation can be, when you simply tune in and embrace the wholeness of who you truly are. Admittedly I've helped you along, particularly during the last eight years, but through your journaling over the past months, you have purged much of your own stagnation. You have cleared the channels so to speak. And now you are ready to fulfill your mission.

How have you been helping me for the last eight years?

Do you remember when you went back to visit the Continent and civilization that you have such a powerful connection with this lifetime?

Egypt! That's when my wife and I went on a three and a half week tour in 1996 with a small group.

That is where we "hooked up".

That was *you*? In the shrine of Sekmet at the temple of Karnak!

Yours truly!

It was almost pitch black in there. We formed a circle and did some "tones" and "om's" during a meditation. Later my wife told me that she opened her eyes during the meditation and saw the outline of a shimmering figure hovering above me. As she watched on—

I slowly descended and merged with you. You have been within my embrace ever since.

But why did I become so ill that same day? During the night show at the temple of Karnak it was as if something suddenly came over me and I spent the next few days in bed.

It was your body reacting to the beginning of the clearing and cleansing process.

Why did it take place in Egypt?

While you were at the temple of Karnak, you experienced many memories of past incarnations. It was the perfect timing to start the transformation. From that time on we have worked together to clear your blocks and to prepare you for your mission and to open your channels for our dialogue.

But what kind of things are we going to talk about? How will it be different to what others have written?

When you go back and read the material of our dialogue to this point, you will realize that our discussion has already covered vast ground. These dialogues are to be complementary to other writings, but it will take concepts and issues relating to the forces of Light and Dark and view them from another perspective. It will be enlightening for many and confronting for some.

But first we must move through the *crunch* factor.

The *crunch* factor?

We've come to the crossroads where you decide whether you take up your destiny's highest potential and continue these conversations, or whether you allow your fears to dictate your future, which will result in the immediate cessation of our dialogue.

—

Do you think you have what it takes this lifetime to continue?

Of course I want the dialogue to continue, but the fear and trepidation I feel at the thought of going public makes me sick to the stomach.

—

73

What if I don't take it up? What will happen to me?

You will live the rest of your life wondering what could have transpired had you accepted the opportunity to move beyond your fears. But don't worry, I'll just come a knock'n at your door next lifetime.

You see, you are in a "free will" zone down here and due to your particular, for want of a better term, self-created patterning of **K**eeping **A R**edundant **M**indset **A**ctualized, it's not a matter of having the choice of *whether* you *will* do it, it's is a matter of having the choice of *when* you *choose* to do it. And don't forget, you've got eternity on your side.

So it's now or never?

It's now or later. Much later.

I'll do it.

I promise you will surprise yourself.

Four

I still don't even really know who you are. All you've given me is an explanation of the Latin term *Lucem Ferre*.

Remember what I said earlier about science concluding that the *nothingness* you can't see when you look up at the night sky makes up more than 90 percent of the entire universe, and that that *something* has been labeled "dark matter"?

Yes.

Metaphorically speaking the meaning of "Lucifer" best describes my true nature, for the universal dichotomy is that *I am* the "dark matter", *I am* Lucifer the "bearer" *of* light, for without my darkness you could not *know* light. *I am* the "birther" *of* light—of the stars, planets, solar systems and entire

75

galaxies—throughout the universe that is *I*. Ultimately *I am* the "womb" of *Creation*; *I am* the womb of my own birthing.

I should really be calling you *Luci*?

Visualize the Chinese symbol of the Yin and the Yang within your mind's eye. Many ancient cultures respected and revered the dark forces as much as they did the light, because they understood that one could not exist without the other. The simplest way to explain is to say that Darkness sits at the right side of Light, as the Light sits at the left side of Darkness. *We* are one; *we* are the complementary polarization of the other.

OMG!

Bingo! You're half way there.

What do you mean "half way" there?

We're getting to the other half.

You expect me to write all this down for the whole world to see? That we got it all wrong? That Lucifer still sits beside God? I'm pretty much "out there" when it comes to this kind of stuff, but your concepts are freaking *me*! Imagine what others will think.

My God'ness, when you get on a roll—

People are going to look at me like I'm some kind of *nutter*! I could be committed! Locked up. Burned at the—

You've been there and done that. For heaven's sake, give people *some* credit! I have just clarified why theologians eradicated the feminine principle from religion, because of their fear of Darkness—the unknown, their internal intuitive self—represented by a symbolic Goddess of Matriarchy. Man had become so detached from his heart that he could no longer find the balance of polarity within himself. And he has been on a fruitless journey searching outside himself for a mythical Holy Grail ever since. That is why on one level he is terrified of "woman", yet she fascinates him. It is why he represses women and why in some cultures within extreme patriarchal regimes, women are excluded from having rights within their society. It is not so long ago that women had no rights within your Western societies.

Man is *afraid of the dark* so to speak, afraid of the feminine principle, of Psyche, of matriarchy and intuition. Why? Because he has dis-empowered, repressed and disowned her existence within himself.

Whether man or woman, we humans have always been "afraid of the dark"!

This is true, however why presume that anything of a spiritual benevolent nature has to be of the light?

Because darkness is associated with evil... scary demons and... monsters!

Does that make "darkness" in itself *bad*?

Well, I suppose putting that way...

Do you not reflect on the beauty of the darkness that reveals the shimmering stars in the evening sky? Are you not birthed from the darkness of your mother's womb? When you feel sad or lost, do you not retreat into the darkness and comfort of your inner self to reflect?
Sometimes, when you lose your way, it is only the solitude of darkness that will light the path back home.

Then why is it everything bad seems to be done under the cover of darkness?

Light is *light*, Dark is *dark*. Consider this: If you chose to become a person with malevolent intention and did not want to be seen, where would you choose to hide—in the light? The most effective means of surprise comes from the sudden appearance from out of the shadow of darkness—that which cannot be seen—that which has yet to be revealed. Does

78

how someone chooses to use darkness in turn make darkness in itself *bad*? Is this really any kind of revelation?

You're telling the story.

Light and Dark are what they are, merely the polarity of each other. You will not hear "judgment" in this statement. How you choose to perceive Mr. L or Mrs. D is up to you, but it does not make either polarity good or bad.

As a dichotomy to your statement, in practical terms "light technology" can be used as a most malevolent and destructive force—just ask anyone who has survived the "flash" from the splitting of the atom in your atomic bomb, or the destructive light-beam of a laser weapon. Does too much light to your eyes not cause you pain?

Don't you think that in my wisdom there is a reason why I created the workings of a solar system that allows for the *lightness* of day and the *darkness* of night? Too much of one or the other in your particular dimension creates imbalance and would be destructive to the cycle of life as you know it. They simply *are* what they *are*.

Did I hear you say, *you* created? So now you're suggesting that I am talking with God?

Earlier it was stated that God, as the Deity and Creator of the universes, is an unfathomable cosmic jewel with infinite facets. I am the *Darkness*, the "womb" from which all things are made manifest. I am the Matriarchal aspect of the Godforce, the feminine principle and *nurturer* of *Creation*, as is *Light* my polarity, the Patriarchal aspect of God, the masculine principle and *provider* of Creation.

Lucifer is the *Goddess* of Creation? You're... our *mother*?

Did I not mention that you would surprise yourself?

"Our *Mother* who art in heaven!" So theologians had it right all along—well at least half right—God *is* our *father*?

Your insight is a beautiful metaphor, but in reality it is all one and the same. The reason we are symbolically talking in terms of gender is because man has shunned the motherly nurturing aspect of the Deity that is "I" for millennia, the pitiful treatment of Mother Nature—and indeed his counterpart that is *woman*—a perfect example of such misguidance. Man's focus, with some exception, has only been on the masculine patriarchal aspect of the Creator for thousands of years—praying to and meditating only on the *one half* of that which he so desires to *fully* comprehend. It is indeed a grand dichotomy!

So the likes of Jesus, Buddha, Krishna, Muhammad and other avatars were truly *Luciferian* in nature? They had found the balance between the light and the dark, between the masculine and feminine within themselves?
They discovered you?

Through the solitude of darkness they were able to rediscover the *bearer of light*, the light of enlightenment within themselves. They found the Holy Grail within because their mind and heart were united. They became the *Bringers of Light* from the darkness within, vessels of information from the higher realms, through the guidance that is *I*.

Bringers of higher knowledge and learning.

Men in particular must rediscover this balance because you cannot come to *know* that which is the Creator merely through the analysis of the mind. This can only be discovered through the feelings of the heart, then in turn the mind will allow for the comprehension of this re-discovery—not the other way round. The Heart is the epicenter, the connection between your linear realm and the higher realms.

But everything we do is based on analysis and intellect. All our wonderful discoveries, inventions and technologies became a reality because of the mind.

Yes, but the *making* of these things could only become a reality from the *application* of intellect and the mind. Where do you think the *idea* came from? The mechanism of the mind can only help sort out and idea or inspiration, but cannot *perceive* the fullness of the *source* unless it is *discovered* through the heart. The mind and the heart, the masculine and the feminine must be brought into balance. This clue is everywhere.

You truly are made in the Creator's image, as is everything within *Creation* a reflection of the *Creator's* imaginings. The workings of your brain are a beautiful example of this polarity.

Your right-brain and its function controls the left side of your body and processes all the attributes from the "inner-internal" feminine principle of Matriarchy, expressed from the "darkness" of your subconscious mind as intuition, creativity and compassion.

In natural harmony your left-brain controls your right side and has all the attributes of the "outer-projection" masculine principles of Patriarchy, expressed through the "light" of your conscious mind as analysis, practicality and action.

WHERE ANGELS FEAR TO TREAD

Once you fully come to this understanding, realization will strike: *Creation* is the child of "our" *duality*—the manifestation of Patriarchy and Matriarchy—working together equally and in harmony *As One*.

From this time forward the term "we", "our" and "us" will be used as a collective description of what you call God or Deity.

As in the royal "we"?

Perfect!

But from what you've just told me, by referring to the Creator as *God* I'm in actual fact only acknowledging the patriarchal aspect, the one half of the total truth. So how should I refer to you... both? I mean... to your *wholeness*? Would it be better if I used the term Creator or Deity?

As you are aware, the Creator does not—in the generally accepted understanding of the term—have a "gender" as such, so it does not matter what title you choose. It is just a word. "God" is a term that has been burned into the psyche of humankind over generations, but from this time forward you can think of God as an omni-conscious presence without feminine or masculine grammatical attributes.

Just like some Western cultures now use the word *actor* to describe the *craft* rather than gender?

Indeed. Think of *God* as a term to describe the *craft* and *essence* of *Creation*.

Just a minute! You nearly had me. You know I love—*used to* love—all this philosophical jargon. But that's in my past. Don't think that just because you've captured my imagination, I'm going to allow you to pull me back in.

Reeling you back in was the easy part. Whether you allow yourself to overcome your preconceived ideas, beliefs and fears from past experiences will be your biggest challenge.

I said I'd do it, didn't I?

Dare we say, "time will tell"?

What do you mean?

Five

Was it something we said?

So, you're still there then?

Well, considering it's over a year ago since you seriously took any real notice, did you not expect we would enquire as to what might have happened?

You mean you don't know? You're the one that said time didn't matter. I've got eternity! Remember?

Yes, you do have eternity. However, when it comes to your particular mission this-time-round, you're nearly out of time.

What do your mean?

You're nearly out of time to fulfill this particular project—

Hang on a minute! How can you tell me I have eternity in one conversation and then that I'm nearly out of time the next?

—this particular lifetime.

But you said—

Everything works in cycles. When you want to fly a mission to Mars, you have to wait for the planets to be in a certain alignment within the solar cycle, so as to catch the window-of-opportunity best suited to fulfill that particular mission within that particular timeframe—a window that will only remain open for an allocated period of time. That is universal law.

Why didn't you tell me this earlier?

Perhaps we could have if you had continued this communication.

So now you're saying I'm about to fail. I'm about to miss out on a window of opportunity yet again?

Not if you decide to jump out of the groove.

Excuse me!

86

The groove in which you're choosing to stay stuck.

What groove?

The "poor me" reruns groove, remember?

Hey! I don't have to take this! I don't even have to talk to you!

Your choosing not to talk to us or not to do anything would not be a failing. It would just be a choice to delay the completion of your mission.

But I didn't know I had a damned choice!

You didn't know?

Well I—

We have already been over this. For years you have known that you have come here with a mission to fulfill, as do many of the souls who will read this book, who will in turn be inspired to jump out of their own re-runs groove of apathy, procrastination and countless other excuses that we hear and have heard every day, every hour and every second of every linear moment since the beginning of time.

87

Did I just detect a tone of judgment and disapproval?

No, it was just a tone—with inflections that clearly activated your own recognition of the above-mentioned facts—of support to help you to realize that if you have changed your mind, it's OK. If you don't want to complete the mission you came down to fulfill this lifetime, it's OK. Just embrace it—own it, state it here, now and forever hold your peace—and we guarantee you, you will not hear from us in this capacity again... this particular lifetime.

I ... I don't want you to leave.

We would never truly *leave* as such, beloved, you would just not hear us again in this capacity this lifetime.

—

Let us go back to the Mars mission. There is no choice in whether the solar system's cycle of the planets can be changed, because universal law dictates their movements. Where the choice lies is in whether you choose to use the window of opportunity that is made available to you within a particular time frame to accomplish the mission.

Your particular window of opportunity, within this particular phase, has nearly, particularly, passed! Will you get over it and get on with it?

I'm kind'a lost for words.

A rather refreshing change, but seriously, how many times have we spoken to you in the last year, and you chose to ignore us? How many situations have we created in your life to remind you to get back to your mission? How many times have you acted as though you were getting back to it by writing a few notes here and there without any real commitment? How many diversions have you created—

ALL RIGHT ALREADY! You've made your point for God's—

Not for God's sake, beloved... for humanity's.

What do you mean?

Fulfilling your mission at this time would provide another piece of the jigsaw that would help to awaken mass-consciousness.

Don't you dare put that pressure on me! I'm not responsible for the rest of humanity.

We are merely bestowing on you the memory of the mission you volunteered to fulfill, the main purpose why you came back.

I don't want that kind of responsibility. Who in their right mind would willingly take something like that on? Who am I anyway! And don't go there again about "the agreement I made before I came back" thing.

Why do you think things haven't worked for you the way you hoped and thought they would? Wasn't that one of the questions in the preamble you scrawled down in anger before these conversations began? Your main service this lifetime is to offer those who are ready a new way to perceive the *wholeness* of The Creator.

So I'm being punished—restricted—because I'm not doing what you want!

There is no punishment. What you perceive as a "restriction" is merely a specific set of parameters that you yourself set in place before you came back, as guideposts to steer you in a direction that will help you fulfill your mission. They are your own creation.

I'm having trouble coming to terms with why I would choose to be come back with a set of restrictions in place.

Do you honestly think you would be writing this now had you achieved any of those things of which you are so desirous? Would you have written your damning preamble to the universe? Would you have gotten yourself into such a state where you would be willing to have a dialogue with Lucifer?

Well, putting it that way... hang on a minute! That's contradictory to your own rules. If this is a "free will" zone, meaning I can choose whatever I want, how could I also have a set of restrictions in place? Do other people have these restrictions?

You continue to choose to perceive your guideposts as a hindrance instead of the support they truly offer. Do you know many people who have been able to create exactly what they want?

No. That's my whole point! For most of us it's a struggle, but there are those who seem to have the Midas Touch! How come they're able to create whatever they want? What makes them so special? Are they working under a different set of rules to the rest of us?

Different people come into life with different sets of parameters to guide them on their journey.

Isn't that the same thing as different "lessons" to be learned?

That term brings with it the connotation of an emotionalized *old school* way of thinking and belongs in the same category as KARMA. You will only have a "lesson to be learned" if it matches your way of thinking.

Can't you allow us all to experience the joy of having the Midas Touch just for a day or two? Then, once we've had a taste it'll give us something to work towards.

Allow us to ask you a question. Do you think humanity has evolved to a level where they can individually handle the responsibility of being able to manifest exactly what they want?

No, obviously not! That's a very scary thought. It would be absolute chaos down here.

Would be?

So why don't you just change the rules for few days, put restrictions on the manifestation parameters… grid… thingy?

The *manifestation rule* has to be the same right across the board; otherwise the rule of *free will* cannot exist. You can't have it both ways.

Yet another set of restrict—

We expect you mean "guideposts"?

—

Let us go back to one of those readings you had a few years ago. It was explained why you couldn't "have-it-all" before you achieved your mission this lifetime. Ring any bells?

Can't hear any at the moment.

Ring! Ring!

Oh so very humorous! If you must know—though, as if you don't already—I was told that in a recent incarnation I achieved my goal of financial abundance and freedom. As a result I supposedly allowed my spiritual obligations and what I'd agreed to fulfill that lifetime fall by the wayside. I think I might have lived it up a touch.

Lived it up a touch! Are you familiar with the word "indulgence"? Perhaps you have forgotten, but in your case, even "debauchery" would be putting it mildly.

You know, I would never have expected you to be so incredibly insensitive and blunt.

Isn't that just how you like it?

93

Some things should remain private. I hadn't planned to share that information with the rest of the world! You have no right—

To show that you are human? Are you telling us you would rather portray yourself—let us borrow from your extensive library of phrases—as some pious *holier-than-thou* servant of the Lord that sets himself up on a pedestal with absolute certainty of falling off?

You're doing it again!

Let us come back to the issue at hand; your recent incarnation where you—and let us pacify your sensitivity on the issue by using your term— "lived it up a touch".

If you were then afforded the opportunity to come back and give it another go, do you think you would firstly consider setting in place a few parameters that might help guide you in a direction that would steer you away from the same fate?

So, if things or certain circumstance are already set in place, how does that afford me "free will"?

That is precisely where "free will" comes in to play, because you instinctively know what you are here to do, and when you follow that "knowing" you are following your higher guidance and guidance

94

posts that have been prepared ahead of your journey. This is when the power of manifestation allows for your hopes, dreams and wishes to become part of your reality, because you are in alignment with your higher purpose... you are in alignment with *us*.

Hopes? Dreams? Wishes? It feels like mine have all withered, died, dried up and been relegated to the hall of broken dreams and dusty records. If we don't live under some kind of restriction down here, then why is it so hard?

Of course you are fundamentally right, you do live within a set of parameters in your particular dimension, however your continued use of the term *restriction* puts this universal truth in a negative light. For one of a better term, this *formula of parameters* makes up the universal law that allows you to experience and exist within the zone of linear time. You could not experience yourself as *"your self"* in a moment-to-moment existence unless there was the opportunity to experience separation; hence, yes, in more than one way *Universal Law* equals "Parameters".

Isn't all that just a nice way of saying that Universal Law equals—

Do you want to stay in the mindset of the *old school* way of thinking—which, by the way hasn't worked for you to date—or are you ready to leave the old groove behind?

You seem to have an answer for everything.

Funny thing that!

What now?

Why did you stop writing a year ago beloved? Why did you hesitate in continuing with our dialogue?

You're the one with all the answers. You know why I stopped writing! Besides, I went overseas for three months—or are you going to tell me you didn't know?

Oh we knew. We were there. We spoke to you while you were at your father's holiday home overlooking the beautiful Lake Balaton in Hungary— a writer's paradise we would have thought—then a week in Budapest, two weeks in Paris, a month roaming round Norway between relatives and finally a week in London.

You blocked us all the way.

Did you really expect me to spend my time writing while I went on the first real holiday I've had in eleven years?

You've been back for over fifteen months.

That's right! And nothing much has changed, has it? I've somehow managed to recreate the same stressful financial situation I was in several years ago! I don't have time to scratch myself. If you're so keen for me to finish this piece of writing, why haven't you helped me? Would one little windfall in Lotto be so hard to arrange, or helping me to make one of my business ideas financially successful?

We didn't realize you held us responsible for your creation. It would seem you're back in that groove again.

Why do you continue to antagonize and humiliate me! Are you trying to push me over the edge?

That is precisely the goal we are endeavoring to help you achieve.

What?

We said earlier—that's over a year ago, by the way—that there was no point jumping off the precipice before you had remembered how to use your wings. While you continue to journal this conversation, your memory is being restored. By the time you have finished you will be healed of your biggest blocks, the anger, the blame and the guilt stored in the fiber of your very cells, finally ready to allow yourself to fly once more.

Why did you stop writing?

OMG! AS IF YOU DON'T KNOW! I had a relapse. I fell back into the damned groove—that black hole of my own personal universe. There! I've admitted to it. Are you happy now?

I remembered why I felt such anger with God and the Creation thing. I didn't feel up to listening to your so-called "words of wisdom" that are somehow supposed to soften the stark reality that that for most people "life sucks"! It all seems like it's just a mental, emotional mind game. I simply don't want to play any more. OK!

I stopped writing because everywhere I went on my travels I saw the same thing over and over again —in one way or another—humanity in a continued state of denial, restriction and let's not forget the pain and suffering thing, whether mental, emotional, physical or all the above. Either way, your little Creationist gameplay seems to have covered every possible option! How can any of it be explained or reasoned through philosophical jargon?

Many more questions have arisen since our last correspondence. Is that why there has been such resistance to getting back to it?

Are you hearing me! I'm outraged at the concept of Creation and the setup here on earth. And that's exactly what it is—it's a bloody *setup*! It's as if there's a program running in the background making sure that life is hard and that every task is a struggle.

I'm on the verge of losing faith in my own philosophy because I can hardly cope with the reality of the pain and anguish that takes place every second of every day in every conceivable corner of the world; countless souls suffering needlessly; men and women fighting wars for the power-mongers that enjoy playing chess with human lives; people being murdered senselessly because of a system that all too often takes from the many only to give to the few; the mental, emotional, physical and sexual abuse of women and children; the devastation caused by nature—the list goes on ad infinitum! And you think all that can be explained away with some namby-pamby philosophical jargon?

How else does it make you feel? Truly vent your emotions.

I feel angry—no, enraged! I'm pissed off with you, dear mother-father God!

How could you have allowed it get to this? How could you have allowed it to get to a point where one of your own creations could feel like this? I've become aware of a feeling of disrespect, verging on condemnation for the Creator, and I know it's because I feel that you have forgotten us.

We know, beloved. But there is more. Continue. We give our blessing.

Your *blessing*! How can you dare to say something like that in response to what I've just said? Is it any wonder it was so easy for the Church to get the populace to believe in a vengeful God so that they in turn became an easy-to-manipulate God-fearing people?

We pray to you! We call to you! We beg you for mercy in our hour of need! Do you really ever answer any of our calls? And I hope your answer is "no", because even if you did why would God only answer some and not others. How can a benevolent God of love and compassion possibly allow any of the horrible things that happen in the world, to take place?

And to this you give your blessing!

The imbalance that has been created in our current reality is the most *unreal* situation imaginable. So why is it that God—the Creator of it all—doesn't stop the pain and suffering in this world of tortured souls? If there were only one metaphor for the crown of thorns on Jesus Christ's head, that would have to be it!

Just where were you when we needed you? Where have you been hiding? Where were you during the atrocities of genocide that were committed against humanity throughout history? Where were you during the Inquisition, while millions were tortured and died at the hand of the Church over the centuries, all because they believed in you from a different viewpoint? Where were you for the countless souls who were fried to a cinder when the Atomic bomb was dropped? WHERE WERE YOU GOD? Why didn't you stop it all?

And where are you when representatives of the Church sexually abuse children in the so-called house of God, when newborn were sacrificed in your name because priests and nuns could not uphold the unrealistic expectation of sexual repression? Where are you when a child is abused by their own parent, relative or so-called friend of the family and when I was molested as a child? Where are you while millions of children in Third World countries die in agony from starvation? Where are you when women are violently abused and raped against their will, while people are violated, murdered and tortured?

Where were you when my mother was being beaten to a pulp, while my brothers and I stood by terrified—images of splattered blood, gaping raw wounds and primal rage burned into the psyche of

101

innocent children—something no one, let alone a child should ever have to endure?

Where were you for the abuser while he stood by as a child watching his father do the same, while he grew up perpetuating his father's deeds because of the helplessness and rage he himself carried? Where were you for him?

Just where the hell are you God during all this mental, emotional and physical torture that is endured down here in this hellhole? Are you just a little too busy in some other corner of the damned universe to answer our call?

OMG! WHY THE HELL HAVE YOU FORSAKEN US? WHERE ARE YOU IN OUR HOUR OF NEED?

Six

We are always there, beloved; we are with you through it all—through every choice that you as co-creators have chosen and continue to choose to perpetuate as your experience—whether you choose to play the role of the oppressed or the oppressor, the inflicted or the inflictor, the innocent or the guilty, we are there with you supporting your choices of *free will* every step of the way.

What do you mean?

These are the extremities under which you yourselves have chosen to create and live out your experiences. This is what you wanted.

Are you telling me this is how God, the Creative Force of the universe, wants to experience itself? In

103

pain and suffering! In constant contradiction? IN A
STATE OF ABSOLUTE INSANITY!

It is not pleasing for *us* to witness or experience
what the co-creators have chosen to manifest in
their, as you put it, *insane* reality. However, because
you, as co-creators, wanted to have the experience
of total "freedom of choice" in a realm without *our,*
shall we call it *assistance*, in this particular dimension,
these are the rules by which all must abide.

To allow for the complete experience of "freedom
of choice" there can be no intervention on a mass
scale, for this would be in direct contradiction of the
rules, the decree that you yourselves have set. And
therein lies the dichotomy of having the *choice* of
choice. The only way we can assist you indirectly is
through our only means of contact—via our co-
creators.

Then why haven't you?

What do you think we are doing here? What do
you think the books you have read are about, the
movies and the plays that affected you so? The
pioneers, the philosophers and avatars revered
throughout your history. They help move you beyond
the limitation of becoming stuck in *beliefs* and
instead help to expand your ideas and the way you
perceive.

But it doesn't help, does it? It's still a crazy, mixed-up place.

Do you know why humanity chooses to remain in this state of insanity?

Please, enlighten me.

If you truly *chose* to live in the *real* world, in a *sane* world—the world that *we intend* for you—you would create nothing less than a *heaven on earth*.

Heaven on earth? That sounds like a far-reaching fantasy! Maybe it's just a bill of goods we've been sold to soften a stark reality.

And what reality is that?

You can't deny that for most people life is a constant struggle in a never-ending uphill battle. Then finally when you come to the top of the mountain where you think you've reached the pinnacle of your life, you find a signpost announcing that in actual fact you have just reached *the end of the road*. And guess what? Your reward, after a lifetime of mental, emotional and physical striving, is to discover that the only way off the mountain is a one way, nonstop plummet to the depths of despair where your ageing decrepit corpse ends up on the scrapheap with the rest of the tortured souls who had to endure the same punishment! And I ask, I beg you to explain, what is the damned point of it all?

A view that clearly falls within the boundary of the pessimist, but since you have spoken in metaphor, let us continue the trend: That *is* the point.

What point!

That a majority of humanity believes they are here under the pretext of *punishment*—the same belief that creates the very reality of pain and suffering from which you so desperately wish to escape.

What has been forgotten is the mission and what must be achieved by the time you get to the top of the metaphoric mountain.

And that is?

When you come to the pinnacle of your life's journey, it is an opportunity for you to awaken—to jump into the void of transcendence.

Transcendence! The pinnacle of life's journey is death?

We were not referring to the ending of your life. We were referring to when you reach a point in your life where you suddenly awaken to a truth and realize you've reached a milestone where everything you once stood for—egoist self-based satisfaction through worldly material possessions, achievements and recognition—isn't so important any more.

This is because by the time you reach what is supposed to be the pinnacle of your life—and if you haven't yet connected with your inner source and guidance—it could be likened to standing at the edge of a precipice ready to take flight, but fear sets in because suddenly you realize you aren't prepared for this day and you've forgotten how to use your wings.

Wings! You're losing me.

In order to soar to the heights of your highest potential, you must firstly remember and relearn how to flex the muscle of your wings—the connection to your angelic or higher self.

Great! So now we're all supposed to turn into a flutter of fairies at the bottom of the garden?

We are talking in symbolic reference. It would be preferable to remember and to reconnect with your higher source, also referred to as your angelic self, before the end of your earthly life. Let us qualify this statement.

When you are born you still remember the freedom of the other realms, and you hold this memory throughout your early years. Observe the children. Does their sense of freedom not remind you of little angels, cherubs awkwardly flitting about, mentally and emotionally unencumbered, not yet fully in command their physical embodiment?

Well, I suppose, if you use your imagination.

They still believe they can fly! If you listen carefully, you will hear the *flutter* of their angelic wings. Have you forgotten your own experience at your grandmother's house?

I think I was about six years old. I remember climbing to the top of the stairs and then jumping, arms outstretched like Superman and floating down to the bottom. But that was a dream. Wasn't it?

Your body may have been asleep, but you brought back the memory of your spirit's freedom to fly, unencumbered by the density of your physical vehicle.

In other words it's not really possible to fly in the physical dimension. I'm sure our genetic programming would show that growing wings was never going to be part of humanities evolution.

Who said you need wings to fly?

—!!

It is your belief system that will not allow you to access the ability to defy gravity at will—and yes, you are correct, it would be a matter of activating *dormant* DNA to achieve this ability.

And it doesn't help that the pressure of "the majority" and belief system of the elders of your clan have usually rendered your instinct to fly a mere fantasy long before you've reached adolescence. You eventually come to believe that such a childish notion is best left as a memory of the past.

Metaphorically speaking, if you listen carefully while around adults, you will also hear the sound of their wings—wings dragged behind them like para-lyzed limbs. You are all angels that have merely forgotten how to fly.

I don't know if I believe in angels anymore.

Your beloved wife recently had an experience during her recovery from an operation that challenges your disbelief.

May I be so bold as to remind you that she was under the influence of drugs at the time. I wouldn't call the ramblings and hallucinations of a patient coming out of anesthesia a very reliable or believable source.

109

The sedative momentarily lowered the veil and helped her to see beyond it. What did she see?

The nurse relayed to her that when she was coming out of the anesthesia in the operating theatre, she told the surgeons and nursing staff that they were all angels.

And?

She described what they looked like.

Yes.

They all had wings.

Don't hold back now. It's so unlike you.

OK! Their wings greatly varied. She described them in detail and explained what their size and color represented. And I got the impression their wings weren't dragging like paralyzed limbs. In fact, I think their wings were... they were...

Their wings were erect. The wings of your angelic self are stronger and more vibrant when you are passionate about your life's purpose and in service to "the greater good".

However, for the sake of sounding cynical, which is also *so* unlike me, I don't remember her saying they flapped their wings and flew round the operating theatre.

Though the ability to physically fly may not yet have been reinstated to most of the human species, "the raising of your angelic wings" image is none-the-less a symbolic indication of your ability to soar to your highest potential. Don't get hung up on this concept of "wings". This manner of speech is merely a way to help you conceptualize your limitless possibility.
That aside, do you realize how uplifted those souls were after having had the privilege of being in your beloved's presence and receiving their due recognition?

I've always considered my wife as an angel in human disguise; particularly with the work she does giving people guidance. Sometimes she finds it very difficult to be down here in this physical realm.

Indeed. She also brought the experience back for you, to help you remember.

I expected you'd weave that in somehow.

Have you listened to the sound of your own wings recently?

I suppose they're dragging behind me like the paralyzed limbs you were talking about. Is it any wonder I feel like I'm weighed down all the time?

You have merely forgotten them because you have allowed yourself to become seduced by your addiction to disappointments.

I have to tell you that I really don't appreciate your flippant remarks.

A flippant remark and a factual statement are two different things. Flippant, we are not.

Is this kind of strategy always part of Archatherapy? Psychological cruelty to the less conscious?

Brutal honesty is your favorite gameplay. Would you really expect us to play the game any differently with you?

Can I sack you?

If you sack us you are sacking yourself.

I think even I'm getting close to admitting defeat! Clearly you're purposefully intending to mentally and emotionally exhaust me! Is torture another part of your strategy?

Breaking down the mental emotional barrier is the only way to get beyond your other self.

My *other self*?

All this time, you don't think we've just been talking with you, do you?

What are you playing at?

Listen carefully...

—

What? I can't hear anyth—

There it is! Did you hear that?

You're losing me.

There it is again! Sounds like there could be a gremlin on the line.

What?

—

Now just hang on a minute! You're plagiarizing the novel I wrote years ago. The "Gremlin" character in my story was just a fantasy, a kind of metaphor for...

For what?

The dark side of human nature.

The *dark* side?

OK, "let us pacify your sensitivity on the issue by using your term" and call it the *shadow* side. After all, "The most effective means of surprise comes from the sudden appearance from out of the shadow of darkness—that which cannot be seen—that which has yet to be revealed." Oh, and by the way, I'm not making a statement, "I am merely paraphrasing".

A good description for that part of your nature that hides in your subconscious—and clearly still appears to be pulling *your* strings, keeping you preoccupied with the dramas of life so that you don't have time to focus on anything that might make you aware of it.

—

Lost for words?

I'm not talking to you.

Do you remember the torture you went through during the time you were writing the manuscript for the novel you started in 1990?

The fact that it took me a while to finish might suggest that it was a touch painful, don't you think?

Why did it take so long?

I'm a slow writer.

And?

I had a lot of research to do.

Why did you go to sleep so often after only 30 minutes of writing?

I had three jobs at the time.

What about the voice?

You know very well I put my singing on hold because—

Not *your* voice, the other voice.

What other voice?

The voice in your head.

Oh! *Your* voice?

You weren't hearing us at the time. The other voice.

I don't remember another voice.

We believe it went something like, *"You're no good at this! Who do you think you are? You're not trained in writing. Stop it now. You're useless at this! No one is going to read this stuff! Accept your station in life! Why do you even bother..."*—

ALRIGHT ALREADY! Why don't you just go ahead and make a subtle point! It was so damned loud in my head that after about 30 minutes of writing, I had to lie down to recover because I was so exhausted from trying to keep my focus above the negativity that I nearly fell unconscious facedown on the keyboard. OK! Are you happy now?

And so what? I got over my negative thoughts and finished it anyway! Even if it did take a few years... or so.

Twelve years, to be precise. What's your reasoning this time round? You've already stretched this conversation out close to five. Perhaps you're trying to break another record.

—

116

So, got over our negative thoughts this time, have we?

Oh, so incredibly witty! I'm just tired of the damned internal criticism. I though I'd written something worthwhile back then, and I published it, but things didn't go how I planned. So what's the point of trying again, only to get the same disappointment?

The dialogue between your main character and the gremlin in that part of your novel wasn't a fantasy. You were talking directly with your shadow self, through the character in your novel.

Whoopee! And now I have to contend with your voice as well. A padded cell and an hourly dose of pills sound like a good remedy to me.

That can be arranged.

Now you listen to me—

We have been listening to your tantrums since you were born. Now it is your turn to listen, but more importantly, to *hear* us. Have you considered the position you find yourself in? Do you fully appreciate the opportunity you have been offered?

No need to yell! You're making me feel like a child being reprimanded by their mother.

Wouldn't that be the most appropriate response from a parent to the child who is behaving like an adolescent? No one is yelling, beloved. It's just that sometimes the blunt truth is painful to hear, particularly for the shadow self.

We will remind you once more. Souls who come here to fulfill a particular mission and accept their obligation also set in place certain criteria and guideposts on their journey to bring them to a point that will remind them that it is their time to act.

Are *you* ready to act?

Not much point having an argument with you, is there?

You are wisely, though be it ever so slowly, coming to that realization. But you have a way to go as yet. Jumping between extremes seems to be your favorite gameplay.

However, had you considered the possibility that I might just be *bipolar,* because I live in a realm of extremes where—as more-or-less described in the dictionary—"participants actively seek out dangerous or even life-threatening experiences to the furthest limit or represents either of the two ends of a scale or range, as an example, the highest or lowest degree of something, or a quality and its *polar* opposite"?

—

Hello? Response required.

—

OK, I'm ready.

You were quite right when you said, "everyday there are countless souls suffering needlessly in this *insane* reality".

Great! Then why hasn't something been done about it?

Because there *is* a program running in the background that works hard at making sure that for most of you, life can be difficult and nearly every task a struggle.

I knew it! Then delete the program. Rewrite it.

Precisely! That is exactly what would be in your best interest.

Excuse me?

We agree.

You agree that…?

119

That something should be done about the old program. It needs rewriting.

Are we getting our wires crossed here? Isn't that what I just asked you—the caring, nurturing matriarchal aspect of God—to do? Aren't you the one that holds the power?

The program that we are speaking of runs in both the *individual* and *collective* mind of humanity. Therefore it can only be deleted or rewritten by the co-creators that actually *created* it—the *collective* human psyche.

So you can't... or you won't change it?

As far as the individual co-creator is concerned, they must choose to make the changes themselves, which *is* taking place through the Mind, Body and Spirit self-awareness and similar New Age movements. Of course, it's not new, it is merely being re-remembered.

That's all very well, but how many attempts have to be made to make the switch, to make the rest of world realize this? More than anyone else, you know that every time someone tries to spread light in this dark place, they're either shot down in—verbal and at times literal—flames, publicly humiliated, persecuted and ridiculed. I'm sure I don't need to remind you, if you make it public that you believe in the principle of equality and goodness for all, you're looked down on as a weak fence-sitting pacifist by the forces that control this place.

They even took the words of some of the greatest avatars our world has seen and then created institutions of patriarchal control to influence the masses, who in turn now believe the only way to salvation is through pain and suffering. And with what you've explained, if "what we think" is in turn actually *charged* by our belief *in* it, which in turn becomes our manifest reality, I believe we are then in turn pretty much—and may I use the *colorful* language-of-current-times—*fucked* before we even start!

And I ask, though the information from those who became enlightened avatars and are now revered in our religions may at times seem profound, what difference has any of it made? What difference did the Love, Peace and Freedom hippy movement of the sixties make, except from what I can gather, everyone got an easy lay!

For that matter, what difference has the Spiritual or New Age movement really made? Maybe it's best if we all just remain in ignorant bliss!

I mean, look around you. In all honesty, do you really see any difference? Isn't the world still bearing up under the brunt of Satan's insatiable desire for pain and suffering—metaphorically speaking, of course—as you've told me he's not real.

All of the *movements* you have mentioned have served their purpose as incremental steps to the next, just the same as our discussion about *codes* of information in books and other types of media being pieces of a jigsaw that will eventually help to complete the full picture. If it were not for these incremental steps, you would currently be living in a very different reality.

Different how?

You have always been fascinated by the prophecies made by the great seers of the past. You have read much of the heavy-duty predictions that forecast a very different scenario from what humanity is currently experiencing, and believe us, the alternative is not a pretty picture. If it were not for all of those things you just mentioned, much of those forecasts would already have been made manifest in your current reality.

I have more questions about predictions and how they work.

We know, however that will be discussed at another time. What must be reiterated here is that when enough of you come to this understanding and a particular "collective" *majority* has made these *program* changes on a personal level, it will create a ripple effect that will change the world as you know it for the better, signs of which are already making themselves evident.

I prefer the idea of the Ascension Process that was promoted years ago. In other words, if you prepared yourself mentally, emotionally and spiritually by a particular time, you would be able to escape from this realm to another realm of love, peace and happiness forever more. What a copout! Made the New Age movement look like an olden time dooms-day sect.

But that *is* your goal.

I beg your pardon?

To achieve ascension—mind and heart united. However, it's not about leaving this realm; it is about becoming the shining example of the *Bearers of Light* that you truly are—by bringing *more* of yourself and your wisdom to the world. That is what the avatars of your past were trying to show you.

For centuries the Covenant of *Lucem Ferre* has remained hidden in the darkness for fear of repercussion by the Institution of Patriarchy that condemned its very existence. Many of you were so devastated by the systematic hunting down and persecution of those who believed in the covenant, that the knowledge of its existence was almost lost.

For centuries souls who aligned themselves with matriarchal covenants have remained hidden within the safety of our cloak-of-darkness, waiting till the way was clear once again.

Your *"cloak-of-darkness"*? I thought a robe of light was the way to protect your self!

—

Oh, I see... darkness in itself isn't bad or good it's more about how you choose to use it... or something like that. Have I covered it?

A robe of light will protect you. However, consider this... a robe of light will also most certainly serve as a beacon of your exact whereabouts at any given time.

Right... I think.

It is now time to own the power of what the founders stood for back in those ancient times and to raise your wings in preparation for flight for the whole world to see.

Metaphorically speaking, of course?

The feminine principle of matriarchy must take its rightful place beside its counterpart of patriarchy to restore the balance. Many of the souls who will read this information will be reminded that it is time to come out where angels fear to tread.

What is it we need to do?

What is it that all sages, avatars and wise ones have preached to those who are seeking the enlightenment of *us* for millennia? And if creating a *heaven on earth* is *our* intention—yet because of the co-creator's free-*will*-choice you are not allowing it to manifest—what exactly do you think it is you need to choose to *let-go-to*?

Are you saying we need to let go... we need to let go to *your will*? Isn't there something about that in the Bible? "Thy will, not my will".

Indeed. *Our will*, will be done on earth as it is in heaven, but only when *we*—that is, *you* and *us* as a *collective will*—allow it to be so. We must be in *uni*-son.

You just love those brain-twisters!
So in simple terms—I can't believe I'm going say this—we need to "let go and let God"?

In more specific terms, it would be in your best interest to let go and let your *higher will* be your guiding light, to align with that part of your

consciousness that is a direct connection to *us*—
"*let go* and *let us*"—*you* and *we* as a collective.

By connecting to the *wholeness* of the Creator,
not just through the analysis of our mind, but
through *heart and mind united*. Isn't that why we
pray and meditate? Yet still I ask, why haven't *we*,
the co-creators, been able to make that happen?

Because, there *is* another *will* at play.

Whose will?

The *will* that stays hidden in the darkness, the
will that keeps the world insane, the *will* that is *not*
"our will".

That all sounds very cryptic! Are you referring to
the shadow self?

Yes, the *will* of the polarized co-creator, the *will*
of the lower ego. But there is another.

It's as if you are referring to a separate evil entity
like Satan.

Your concept of Satan is merely a figurehead,
an image that has been created to represent the
will of the 'mass-conscious' shadow or lower ego—

the creature of your imagination that lurks about in the darkness of your subconscious mind.

Like a virus in a computer that causes havoc with your manifestation program.

Indeed. The program of KARMA will only play a part in your reality if it is fed and charged with your belief.

Keeping **A R**edundant **M**indset **A**ctualized! Now I get it. It was just a classic case of projection, someone to blame for our hardships? That's no different to the religious effigies used by ancient cultures throughout history.

This fear-induced *will* of mass-consciousness is represented by a malevolent satanic figurehead, just as the concept of a benevolent God is represented by an old-bearded guy sitting on a throne.

That's because church authorities wanted us to behave like good little children. What hope did we have when even God was sold as a character to be feared, as evidenced in the *Wrath of God* scenario!

And so, what you're saying about Satan is… that it's all made up?

Yes. It is simply our newfound interpretation of KARMA.

So if we, your co-creators, believe in Satan as an entity, we're actually keeping a negative limitation-virus in our minds alive?

Couldn't have put it better.

I get that, but if there's no such thing as Satan... hang on a minute. If there's no such thing as Satan, being the representative of evil and *badness*... and it's *all* made up by KARMA... then couldn't you also say there's no such a thing as its opposite—God representing love and goodness?

Exactly.

What *exactly* are you trying to do to my brain function here?

The Good and Bad thing is all made up. It is merely a conceptualized belief system that you have set in place to help you understand the extremes of the parameters within which you live while you are in embodiment locked within a polarized reality. But in reality, they are simply *beliefs* that are energizing and Keeping **A** **R**edundant **M**indset **A**ctualized.

So what *is God* then?

God is *Neutral*—neither Good nor Bad—God just *is*.

128

I don't think I like this conversation any more.

That's because it is challenging the very core of your belief system. Don't misunderstand our statement... while you are a polarized being and perceive yourself as separate from God, when you are in God's presence, you will continue to experience all those good, nice and loving things that you perceive about *us*, just not from an emotionalized standpoint. But in our purest form, *We* are *Neutral: We* just *are*.

What about the program you were talking about, the voice in my head, the lower ego trying to undermine me, the mass conscious *will* represented by a fictitious character called Satan, all the concepts of KARMA and the changing the program thing? Why do we need to change it if it's not real?

It is not real in the sense that it was not created by *us* as a means of a reward and punishment system for deeds done. It only seems real for you and is experienced by you as long as you continue to feed or energize it with your *belief*.

By **K**eeping **A** **R**edundant **M**indset **A**ctualized.

Precisely. It is merely a program, a program that can be deleted, de-energized and de-commissioned by your disconnecting it from its energy source—your *belief* in it. This will ripple through the **Q**uantum **P**hysics **M**atrix like a wave of energy that will transmute and cleanse any KARMA virus present within it.

The What! "Quantum Physics Matrix"?

The QPM is the *motherboard*, the spiritual, metaphysical technology that allows you to experience and to be present within your current reality, within what your sciences have termed the physical or third dimension.

Are you going to tell us in more detail how the QPM works and how to delete the KARMA virus?

That is our intention.

Something struck me since you referred to God as being *neutral*. The theological concept of "Lucifer being thrown out of heaven" and the "falling from grace" thing has puzzled me for some time.

We know.

From what I can remember from Sunday school, in theology Archangel Lucifer, portrayed as a male, was thrown out of heaven because he disobeyed God. And I think it was Archangel Michael that had a hand in removing Lucifer from heaven. So if God is at the centre of it all—in a *neutral* state—it seems this somehow refers to the Creationist concept of good and evil, but I can't quite get my brain round it.

You are almost there. In this scenario the early theologians inadvertently and symbolically described the true nature of Creation. To begin the process, part of God's *neutral* state had to be polarized to generate two "opposite" *states of being*. The variance between the two allowed for the development of separated or individual states of consciousness' that in turn allowed for the experience of *self*-awareness.

In simple terms, Lucifer represents Dark, the feminine so-called "negative" *charge* of Matriarchy, while Michael represents Light, the masculine so-called "positive" *charge* of Patriarchy, but without the connotation of Bad or Good attached to those descriptions; that was later added from an emotional-ized human standpoint and perception.

The *polarization* of God? Are you referring to The Big Bang?

Indeed!

OMG!

Why The Hell Have You Forsaken Us?

ONE HELL'UVA BIG BANG!

BY

Jêan Németh

Available early 2013

**To be notified of release please email
wakemanpublishing@jeannemeth.com**

About The Author

Jêan Németh was born in Norway and moved to Australia with his family at the age of ten. His interests leaned towards the creative arts and one of his favorite subjects at school was creative writing. By his mid teens he turned his attention to music, spending many years training in classical singing. He sang with the Victoria State Opera company ensemble for several years during the 90's and also freelanced with Opera Australia's ensemble during this time. While he had a break from music he developed an interest in environmental issues, the psychological, philosophical and spiritual aspects of the human condition and in metaphysical and esoteric subjects. He is currently working on *OMG! Why the hell have you forsaken us? - One Hell'uva big Bang!* and is preparing his original novel *The Shift of the Ages* for a re-release late 2012. Jêan is also in the process of developing a CD of original songs and covers.

For further information and updates please visit
www.JeanNemeth.com

COMING SOON

THE SHIFT
OF THE AGES

A NOVEL BY

Jêan Németh

According to the ancient Mayan Calendar the world as we know
it will end December 21 2012

The ancients referred to it as The Shift Of The Ages

Where will you be?
With your family... with friends... with your lover?

Jake Wakeman, an unsung hero of the New World will be
alone... at the top of a sky-scraper in preparation to try and
alter the outcome of a cataclysmic Mayan prophecy. Come join
him in this spirited fast-paced adventure and discover what
really lies beyond The Shift Of The Ages.

Digital Release
AVAILABLE OCTOBER 2012

To be notified please email
wakemanpublishing@jeannemeth.com

www.ingramcontent.com/pod-product-compliance
Lightning Source LLC
Chambersburg PA
CBHW071001040426
42443CB00007B/613